Python Asyncio Jump-Start

Asynchronous Programming And Non-Blocking I/O With Coroutines

Jason Brownlee

2022

Praise for *SuperFast*Python

"I'm reading this article now, and it is really well made (simple, concise but comprehensive). Thank you for the effort! Tech industry is going forward thanks also by people like you that diffuse knowledge."

– **Gabriele Berselli**, Python Developer.

"I enjoy your postings and intuitive writeups - keep up the good work"

– **Martin Gay**, Quantitative Developer at Lacima Group.

"Great work. I always enjoy reading your knowledge based articles"

– **Janath Manohararaj**, Director of Engineering.

"Great as always!!!"

– **Jadranko Belusic**, Software Developer at Crossvallia.

"Thank you for sharing your knowledge. Your tutorials are one of the best I've read in years. Unfortunately, most authors, try to prove how clever they are and fail to educate. Yours are very much different. I love the simplicity of the examples on which more complex scenarios can be built on, but, the most important aspect in my opinion, they are easy to understand. Thank you again for all the time and effort spent on creating these tutorials."

– **Marius Rusu**, Python Developer.

"Thanks for putting out excellent content Jason Brownlee, tis much appreciated"

– **Bilal B.**, Senior Data Engineer.

"Thank you for sharing. I've learnt a lot from your tutorials, and, I am still doing, thank you so much again. I wish you all the best."

– **Sehaba Amine**, Research Intern at LIRIS.

"Wish I had this tutorial 7 yrs ago when I did my first multithreading software. Awesome Jason"

– **Leon Marusa**, Big Data Solutions Project Leader at Elektro Celje.

"This is awesome"

– **Subhayan Ghosh**, Azure Data Engineer at Mercedes-Benz R&D.

Copyright

Disclaimer

Preface

Python concurrency is deeply misunderstood.

Opinions vary from *"Python does not support concurrency"* to *"Python concurrency is buggy"*.

I created the website SuperFastPython.com to directly counter these misunderstandings.

Asyncio is a new, important, and exciting addition to Python.

Broadly, asyncio refers to changes to the Python language to support coroutines, and the `asyncio` module that provides an API for developing and running programs using coroutines with an asynchronous programming style.

Asyncio was added specifically to support non-blocking I/O with socket connections. Combined with asynchronous programming, this is typically referred to as asynchronous I/O.

Using asyncio, we can develop programs that exceed the scalability of threads, allowing tens or hundreds of thousands of concurrent streams. This capability can be used to develop client-side or server-side programs that access a vast number of concurrent TCP socket connections, perhaps to servers, websites, game servers, databases, and more.

This guide was carefully designed to help Python developers (*like you*) to get productive with asyncio as fast as possible. After completing all seven lessons, you will know how to bring coroutine-based concurrency with the `asyncio` module API to your own projects, super fast.

Together, we can make Python code run faster and change the community's opinions about Python concurrency.

Thank you for letting me guide you along this path.

Jason Brownlee, Ph.D.
SuperFastPython.com
2022.

Contents

Introduction

The `asyncio` module allows us to develop asynchronous I/O programs using coroutines in Python.

Coroutines are a different unit of concurrency from threads and processes. The Python language was expanded to provide coroutines with specialized expressions such as `async`/`await`.

Coroutines are suited to the asynchronous programming paradigm, and asynchronous programming is well suited to programs that read and write from resources in a non-blocking manner, called non-blocking or asynchronous I/O.

This book provides a jump-start guide to get you productive with developing asyncio programs.

It is not a dry, long-winded academic textbook. Instead, it is a crash course for Python developers that provides carefully designed lessons with complete and working code examples that you can copy-paste into your project today and get results.

Before we dive into the lessons, let's look at what is coming with a breakdown of this book.

Who Is This For

Before we dive in, let's make sure you're in the right place.

This book is designed for Python developers who want to discover how to use and get the most out of the `asyncio` module to write

1

fast programs.

Specifically, this book is for:

- Developers that can write simple Python programs.
- Developers that need better performance from current or future Python programs.
- Developers that are working with I/O-based tasks.

This book does not require that you are an expert in the Python programming language or concurrency.

Specifically:

- You do not need to be an expert Python developer.
- You do not need to be an expert in concurrency.

Next, let's take a look at what this book will cover.

Book Overview

This book is designed to bring you up-to-speed with how to use asyncio as fast as possible.

As such, it is not exhaustive. There are many topics that are interesting or helpful but are not on the critical path to getting you productive fast.

This book is divided into a course of 7 lessons, they are:

- **Lesson 01**: Asyncio Concurrency
- **Lesson 02**: Coroutines and Tasks
- **Lesson 03**: Collections of Tasks
- **Lesson 04**: Iterators, Generators, and Context Managers
- **Lesson 05**: Queues and Synchronization Primitives
- **Lesson 06**: Subprocesses and Streams
- **Lesson 07**: Port Scanner Case Study

Next, let's take a closer look at how lessons are structured.

Lesson Structure

Each lesson has two main parts, they are:

1. The body of the lesson.
2. The lesson overview.

The body of the lesson will introduce a topic with code examples, whereas the lesson overview will review what was learned with exercises and links for further information.

Each lesson has a specific learning outcome and is designed to be completed in less than one hour.

Each lesson is also designed to be self-contained so that you can read the lessons out of order if you choose, such as dipping into topics in the future to solve specific programming problems.

The lessons were written with some intentional repetition of key concepts. These gentle reminders are designed to help embed the common usage patterns in your mind so that they become second nature.

We Python developers learn best from real and working code examples.

Next, let's learn more about the code examples provided in the book.

Code Examples

All code examples use Python 3.

Python 2.7 is not supported because it reached its end of life in 2020.

I recommend the most recent version of Python 3 available at the time you are reading this, although Python 3.9 or higher is sufficient to run all code examples in this book.

You do not require any specific integrated development environment (IDE). I recommend typing code into a simple text editor like Sublime Text or Atom that run on all modern operating systems. I'm a

Sublime user myself, but any text editor will do. If you are familiar with an IDE, then, by all means, use it.

Each code example is complete and can be run as a standalone program. I recommend running code examples from the command line (also called the command prompt on Windows or terminal on macOS) to avoid any possible issues.

To run a Python script from the command line:

1. Save the code file to a directory of your choice with a `.py` extension.
2. Open your command line (also called the command prompt or terminal).
3. Change the directory to the location where you saved the Python script.
4. Execute the script using the Python interpreter followed by the name of the script.

For example:

```
python my_script.py
```

I recommend running scripts on the command line. It is easy, it works for everyone, it avoids all kinds of problems that beginners have with notebooks and IDEs, and scripts run fastest on the command line.

That being said, if you know what you're doing, you can run code examples within your IDE or a notebook if you like. Editors like Sublime Text and Atom will let you run Python scripts directly, and this is fine. I just can't help you debug any issues you might encounter because they're probably caused by your development environment.

All lessons in this book provide code examples. These are typically introduced first via snippets of code that begin with an ellipsis (. . .) to clearly indicate that they are not a complete code example. After the program is introduced via snippets, a complete code example is always listed that includes all of the snippets tied together, with any additional glue code and import statements.

I recommend typing code examples from scratch to help you learn and memorize the API.

Beware of copy-pasting code from the EBook version of this book as you may accidentally lose or add white space, which may break the execution of the script.

A code file is provided for each complete example in the book organized by lesson and example within each lesson. You can execute these scripts directly or use them as a reference.

You can download all code examples from here:

- Download Code Examples
  https://SuperFastPython.com/paj-code

All code examples were tested on a POSIX machine by myself and my technical editors prior to publication.

APIs can change over time, functions can become deprecated, and idioms can change and be replaced. I keep this book up to date with changes to the Python standard library and you can email me any time to get the latest version. Nevertheless, if you encounter any warnings or problems with the code, please contact me immediately and I will fix it. I pride myself on having complete and working code examples in all of my lessons.

Next, let's learn more about the exercises provided in each lesson.

Practice Exercises

Each lesson has an exercise.

The exercises are carefully designed to test that you understood the learning outcome of the lesson.

I strongly recommend completing the exercise in each lesson to cement your understanding.

NOTE: I recommend sharing your results for each exercise publicly.

This can be done easily using social media sites like Twitter, Facebook, and LinkedIn, on a personal blog, or in a GitHub project. Include the name of this book or SuperFastPython.com to give context to your followers.

I recommend sharing your answers to exercises for three reasons:

- It will improve your understanding of the topic of the lesson.
- It will keep you accountable, ensuring you complete the lesson to a high standard.
- I'd love to see what you come up with!

You can email me the link to your answer for each exercise directly via:

- Super Fast Python - Contact Page
  https://SuperFastPython.com/contact/

Or share it with me on Twitter via @SuperFastPython.

Next, let's consider how we might approach working through this book.

How to Read

You can work at your own pace.

There's no rush and I recommend that you take your time.

This book is designed to be read linearly from start to finish, guiding you from being a Python developer at the start of the book to being a Python developer that can confidently use the `asyncio` module in your project by the end of the book.

In order to avoid overload, I recommend completing one or two lessons per day, such as in the evening or during your lunch break. This will allow you to complete the transformation in about one week.

I recommend maintaining a directory with all of the code you type from the lessons in the book. This will allow you to use the directory as your own private code library, allowing you to copy-paste code into your projects in the future.

I recommend trying to adapt and extend the examples in the lessons. Play with them. Break them. This will help you learn more about how the API works and why we follow specific usage patterns.

Next, let's review your newfound capabilities after completing this book.

Learning Outcomes

This book will transform you from a Python developer into a Python developer that can confidently bring concurrency to your projects with asyncio.

After working through all of the lessons in this book, you will know:

- How to define, create, and run coroutines and how to use the `async`/`await` expressions.
- How to create asynchronous tasks, query their status, cancel them and add callback functions.
- How to run many coroutines concurrently in a group and handle their results.
- How to wait for many coroutines to complete, meet a condition, or timeout.
- How to define, create and use asynchronous iterators, generators, and context managers.
- How to use the `async for` and `async with` expressions in asyncio programs.
- How to synchronize and coordinate coroutines with locks, semaphores, events and condition variables.
- How to share data between coroutines using coroutine-safe queues.
- How to run, read, and write from subprocesses and streams with coroutines.
- How to develop a concurrent and dynamically updating port scanner using non-blocking I/O.

Next, let's discover how we can get help when working through the book.

Getting Help

The lessons in this book were designed to be easy to read and follow.

Nevertheless, sometimes we need a little extra help.

A list of further reading resources is provided at the end of each lesson. These can be helpful if you are interested in learning more about the topic covered, such as fine-grained details of the standard library and API functions used.

The conclusions at the end of the book provide a complete list of websites and books that can help if you want to learn more about Python concurrency and the relevant parts of the Python standard library. It also lists places where you can go online and ask questions about Python concurrency.

Finally, if you ever have questions about the lessons or code in this book, you can contact me any time and I will do my best to help. My contact details are provided at the end of the book.

Now that we know what's coming, let's get started.

Next

Next up in the first lesson, we will discover coroutine-based concurrency with asyncio in Python.

Lesson 01: Asyncio Concurrency

In this lesson, we will explore asyncio, including coroutines, asynchronous programming and the `asyncio` module. We will develop an asyncio *hello world* program and understand how it works.

After completing this lesson, you will know:

- What is a coroutine and how it relates to subroutines, threads, and generators.
- What is asynchronous programming and asynchronous I/O.
- What the `asyncio` module is and the capabilities it provides.
- How to develop a *hello world* asyncio program and know how it works.
- When to use asyncio in your programs.

Let's get started.

What are Coroutines

A coroutine is a function that can be suspended and resumed.

It is often defined as a generalized subroutine.

A subroutine is a function that can be executed, starting at one point and finishing at another point. Whereas, a coroutine can be executed then suspended, and resumed many times before finally terminating.

Specifically, coroutines have control over when exactly they suspend their execution.

This may involve the use of a specific expression, such as an `await` expression, or like a `yield` expression in a generator.

A coroutine may suspend for many reasons, such as executing another coroutine, e.g. awaiting another task, or waiting for some external resources, such as a socket connection or process to return data.

Coroutines are used for concurrency.

Many coroutines can be created and executed at the same time. They have control over when they will suspend and resume, allowing them to cooperate as to when concurrent tasks are executed.

This is called cooperative multitasking and is different to the multitasking typically used with threads called preemptive multitasking.

Preemptive multitasking involves the operating system choosing what threads to suspend and resume and when to do so, as opposed to the tasks themselves deciding in the case of cooperative multitasking.

Now that we have some idea of what a coroutine is, let's deepen this understanding by comparing them to other familiar programming constructs.

Coroutine vs Routine and Subroutine

A *routine* and *subroutine* often refer to the same thing in modern programming.

Perhaps more correctly, a routine is a program, whereas a subroutine is a function in the program.

A routine has subroutines.

It is a discrete module of expressions that is assigned a name, may take arguments and may return a value.

- **Subroutine**: A module of instructions that can be executed on demand, typically named, and may take arguments and return a value. Also called a function.

A subroutine is executed, runs through the expressions, and returns somehow. Typically, a subroutine is called by another subroutine.

A coroutine is an extension of a subroutine. This means that a subroutine is a special type of coroutine.

A coroutine is like a subroutine in many ways, such as:

- They both are discrete named modules of expressions.
- They both can take arguments, or not.
- They both can return a value, or not.

The main difference is that a coroutine chooses to suspend and resume its execution many times before returning and exiting.

Both coroutines and subroutines can call other examples of themselves. A subroutine can call other subroutines. A coroutine executes other coroutines. However, a coroutine can also execute other subroutines.

When a coroutine executes another coroutine, it must suspend its execution and allow the other coroutine to run.

This is like a subroutine calling another subroutine. The difference is the suspension of the coroutine may allow any number of other coroutines to run as well.

This makes a coroutine calling another coroutine more powerful than a subroutine calling another subroutine. It is central to the cooperative multitasking facilitated by coroutines.

Next, let's look at how coroutines are related to generators.

Coroutine vs Generator

A generator is a special function that can suspend its execution.

A generator function can be defined like a normal function although it uses a `yield` expression at the point it will suspend its execution and return a value.

A generator function will return a generator iterator object that can be traversed, such as via a for-loop. Each time the generator is executed, it runs from the last point it was suspended to the next `yield` expression.

A coroutine can suspend or `yield` to another coroutine using an `await` expression. It will then resume from this point once the awaited coroutine has been completed.

We can think of a generator as a special type of coroutine and cooperative multitasking used in loops.

Before coroutines were developed, generators were extended so that they can be used like coroutines in our programs.

This required a lot of technical knowledge of generators and the development of custom task schedulers.

This was made possible via changes to the generators and the introduction of the `yield from` expression.

These were later deprecated in favor of the modern `async/await` expressions.

Next, let's look at how coroutines are different to threads.

Coroutine vs Thread

A thread refers to a thread of execution in a computer program.

Each program is a process and has at least one thread that executes instructions for that process.

When we run a script, it starts an instance of the interpreter that runs our code in the main thread. The main thread is the default thread of a process.

The underlying operating system controls how new threads are created, when threads are executed, and which CPU core executes them.

A coroutine is more lightweight than a thread.

A coroutine is defined as a function, whereas a thread is an object created and managed by the underlying operating system and represented as a `threading.Thread` object.

- **Thread**: Unit of concurrency managed by the operating system, represented by an object. Belongs to a process, may execute many coroutines.

This means that coroutines are typically faster to create and start executing and take up less memory. Conversely, threads are slower than coroutines to create and start and take up more memory.

Coroutines execute within one thread, therefore a single thread may execute many coroutines.

Now that we are familiar with coroutines, let's look at asynchronous programming.

What is Asynchronous Programming

In this section, we will discover asynchronous programming and how it relates to asynchronous I/O.

Before we dive into asynchronous programming, let's understand what *asynchronous* means.

What is Asynchronous

Asynchronous means not at the same time, as opposed to synchronous or at the same time.

When programming, asynchronous means that the action is requested, although not performed at the time of the request. It is performed later.

For example, we can make an asynchronous function call.

This will issue the request to make the function call and will not wait around for the call to complete. We can choose to check on the status or result of the function call later.

- **Asynchronous Function Call**: Request that a function is called at some time and in some manner, allowing the caller to resume and perform other activities.

The function call will happen somehow and at some time, in the background, and the program can perform other tasks or respond to other events.

This is key. We don't have control over how or when the request is handled, only that we would like it handled while the program does other things.

Issuing an asynchronous function call often results in some handle on the request that the caller can use to check on the status of the call or get results. This is often called a future.

- **Future**: A handle on an asynchronous function call allowing the status of the call to be checked and results to be retrieved.

The combination of the asynchronous function call and future together is often referred to as an asynchronous task. This is because it is more elaborate than a function call, such as allowing the request to be canceled and more.

- **Asynchronous Task**: Used to refer to the aggregate of an asynchronous function call and resulting future.

Issuing asynchronous tasks and making asynchronous function calls is referred to as asynchronous programming.

- **Asynchronous Programming**: The use of asynchronous techniques, such as issuing asynchronous tasks or function calls.

We now have the building blocks to consider asynchronous I/O.

What is Asynchronous I/O

Asynchronous programming is primarily used with non-blocking I/O, such as reading and writing from socket connections with other processes or other systems.

Non-blocking I/O is a way of performing I/O where reads and writes are requested, although performed asynchronously. The caller does not need to wait for the operation to complete before returning.

The read and write operations are performed somehow (e.g. by the underlying operating system or systems built upon it), and the status of the action and/or data is retrieved by the caller later, once available, or when the caller is ready.

- **Non-blocking I/O**: Performing I/O operations via asynchronous requests and responses, rather than waiting for operations to complete.

As such, we can see how non-blocking I/O is related to asynchronous programming. In fact, we use non-blocking I/O via asynchronous programming.

The combination of non-blocking I/O with asynchronous programming is so common that it is referred to by the shorthand of asynchronous I/O.

- **Asynchronous I/O**: A shorthand that refers to combining asynchronous programming with non-blocking I/O.

Next, let's consider asynchronous programming support in Python.

Asynchronous Programming in Python

Broadly, asynchronous programming in Python refers to making requests and not blocking to wait for them to complete.

We can implement asynchronous programming in Python in various ways.

The first and obvious example is the `asyncio` module.

This module directly offers an asynchronous programming environment using the `async/await` syntax and non-blocking I/O with sockets and subprocesses.

It is implemented using coroutines that run in an event loop that itself runs in a single thread.

- **Asyncio**: An asynchronous programming environment provided in Python via the `asyncio` module.

We will learn more about this module in the next section.

More broadly, Python offers threads and processes that can execute tasks asynchronously.

For example, one thread can start a second thread to execute a function call and resume other activities. The operating system will schedule and execute the second thread at some time and the first thread may or may not check on the status of the task, manually.

More concretely, Python provides `Executor`-based thread pools and process pools in the `ThreadPoolExecutor` and `ProcessPoolExecutor` classes.

These classes use the same interface and support asynchronous tasks via the `submit()` method that returns a `Future` object.

The `multiprocessing` module also provides pools of workers using processes and threads in the `Pool` and `ThreadPool` classes, forerunners to the `ThreadPoolExecutor` and `ProcessPoolExecutor` classes.

The capabilities of these classes are described in terms of worker execution tasks asynchronously. They explicitly provide synchronous (blocking) and asynchronous (non-blocking) versions of each method for executing tasks.

For example, one may issue a one-off function call synchronously via the `apply()` method or asynchronously via the `apply_async()` method.

This highlights that although we are focused on asynchronous programming with coroutines and `asyncio` module, that Python provides alternate ways to develop asynchronous programs.

Now that we are familiar with coroutines and asynchronous programming, let's finally look at asyncio.

Welcome to Asyncio

Python provides coroutines as first-class objects and the `asyncio` module supports asynchronous programming.

Asynchronous programming in Python using coroutines and the `asyncio` module is typically referred to simply as *asyncio*.

Nevertheless, it is helpful to separate these concerns, at least initially, so we can better understand them.

Coroutines in Python

Python supports coroutines directly via additions to the language, including new expressions and types.

A coroutine can be defined via the `async def` expression.

This is an extension of the `def` expression for defining subroutines.

It defines a coroutine that can be created and returns a coroutine object.

For example:

```
# define a coroutine
async def custom_coro():
    # ...
```

A coroutine defined with the `async def` expression is referred to as a *coroutine function*.

Calling a coroutine function will return a coroutine object, which is an instance of the `coroutine` class, a type provided in the Python language.

A coroutine can then use coroutine-specific expressions within it, such as `await`, `async for`, and `async with`.

The `await` expression will suspend the calling coroutine and schedule the specified coroutine to execute. The caller will not resume until the specified coroutine is done.

For example:

```
# define a coroutine
async def custom_coro():
    # await another coroutine
    await another_coro()
```

This was just a taste of coroutines in Python, we will learn more about how to define, create and run coroutines in *Lesson 02: Coroutines and Tasks*,

Next, let's learn more about the `asyncio` module.

The `asyncio` Module

Python supports asynchronous programming directly via the `asyncio` module.

The module provides utility functions and classes to assist in creating and managing asynchronous tasks and performing non-blocking I/O with sockets and subprocesses.

It also provides utility functions to simulate non-blocking tasks with blocking I/O and CPU-bound tasks using thread pools and process pools under the covers.

Critically, it provides the event loop required to execute coroutines.

Coroutines can be defined and created, but they can only be executed within an event loop. The event loop that executes coroutines, manages the cooperative multitasking between coroutines. It is also responsible for executing callback functions and managing the non-blocking network I/O.

In asyncio applications, we don't need to interact directly with the asyncio event loop, other than starting it. Nevertheless, there is a low-level API for getting access to the event loop object and methods for interacting with it.

The way to start the asyncio event loop is via the `asyncio.run()` function.

This function takes one coroutine and returns the value of the coroutine. The provided coroutine can be used as the entry point into the coroutine-based program. I like to call it the *main coroutine*, similar to the main thread and main process in other forms of concurrency.

For example:

```
...
# start an asyncio program
asyncio.run(main())
```

In addition to the event loop infrastructure, the `asyncio` module provides many high-level features for using our asynchronous programs, such as:

- Utility functions for creating and scheduling asynchronous tasks.
- Functions and classes for opening and managing non-blocking TCP socket connections.
- Functions and classes for starting and managing non-blocking subprocesses.
- Synchronization primitives for encouraging coroutine safety.
- Coroutines-safe queues for message passing between coroutines.

Now that we have seen how Python supports coroutines and the `asyncio` module supports developing coroutine-based asynchronous programming, let's look at a worked example.

Asyncio Hello World Example

The first program we write in a new programming language is a *hello world* program.

The `asyncio` module is different from most other modules.

Using it is like writing code in a new programming language. It's different from *normal* programming.

It is the reason why so many developers are excited to use it, and why others are afraid to get started.

The first step into asyncio is to write a hello world. The second step is to understand what it does.

Asyncio Hello World

Let's write a hello world for asyncio.

The complete example is listed below.

Type the example and run it, or copy-paste it.

This is our first step on the asyncio journey.

```python
# SuperFastPython.com
# example of a hello world program for asyncio
import asyncio

# define a coroutine
async def custom_coroutine():
    # report a message
    print('Hello world')

# execute the coroutine
asyncio.run(custom_coroutine())
```

Running the example reports the *hello world* message.

```
Hello world
```

Full of questions? Good!

Now, let's slow everything down and understand what this example does.

Asyncio Hello World in Detail

We know how to type and run a hello world for asyncio, now let's understand what it does (at least from a birds-eye view).

What should a hello world program for asyncio do?

If asyncio is for coroutine-based concurrency, we should create and run a coroutine.

If we were exploring thread-based concurrency in the **threading** module, we would create and run a thread. This would be the same if we were exploring process-based concurrency in the **multiprocessing** module.

Recall, a subroutine is a function. For example, we can define a function to print hello world as follows:

```
# custom routine
def custom_routine():
    # report a message
    print('Hello world')
```

A coroutine is a function that can be suspended.

We can define a coroutine just like a normal function, except it has the added **async** keyword before the **def** keyword.

For example:

```
# define a coroutine
async def custom_coroutine():
    # report a message
    print('Hello world')
```

So far, so good.

We cannot execute a coroutine like a subroutine.

If we call our **custom_coroutine** directly, we get warning messages that look like an error.

For example:

```
# SuperFastPython.com
# example of calling a coroutine directly

# define a coroutine
async def custom_coroutine():
```

```
    # report a message
    print('Hello world')

# call the coroutine directly
custom_coroutine() # raises warning
```

Running the example results in warning messages that look scary.

The first says that we never *awaited* our coroutine.

The second is not at all helpful.

```
...
RuntimeWarning: coroutine '...' was never awaited
    custom_coroutine()
RuntimeWarning: Enable tracemalloc to get the object
    allocation traceback
```

We cannot call a coroutine directly.

Instead, we must have the routine called for us by the asyncio run time, called the event loop.

This can be achieved by calling the `asyncio.run()` module function.

This function will start the asyncio event loop in the current thread, and we can only have one of these running in a thread at a time.

It takes a coroutine as an argument.

Not the name of the coroutine, like the `target` argument of a `threading.Thread` or `multiprocessing.Process`, instead it takes an instance of a coroutine.

We can create an instance of a coroutine just like creating an object, and it looks like we are calling the coroutine.

For example:

```
...
# execute the coroutine
asyncio.run(custom_coroutine())
```

This will start the event loop and execute the coroutine and print the message.

But, let's unpack this further.

If we are creating an instance of a coroutine and passing it to the `asyncio.run()` module function to execute, why not assign it first?

For example:

```
...
# create the coroutine and assign it to a variable
coro = custom_coroutine()
# execute the coroutine
asyncio.run(coro)
```

This makes more sense now.

We can clearly see the creation of the coroutine and it is passed to the `asyncio.run()` function for execution.

There's one more thing.

If we don't execute an instance of a coroutine, we will get a warning.

This means that if we create and assign an instance of our custom coroutine and do not pass it to `asyncio.run()`, a warning message is reported.

For example:

```
# SuperFastPython.com
# example of creating but not awaiting a coroutine

# define a coroutine
async def custom_coroutine():
    # report a message
    print('Hello world')

# create the coroutine and assign it to a variable
coro = custom_coroutine() # raises warning
```

Running the example creates the coroutine, but does not do anything with it.

The runtime then reports this as a warning message, similar to what we saw when we called the coroutine directly.

```
sys:1: RuntimeWarning: coroutine '...' was never awaited
```

So now we know what our hello world example does. We will go into more detail in later lessons.

Now that we have seen our first coroutine and asyncio program, let's look at when we should use asyncio, and when we shouldn't.

When to Use Asyncio

There are perhaps three top reasons to adopt asyncio in a project, they are:

- The non-blocking I/O with subprocesses or socket connections is required.
- The benefits of coroutines outweigh the benefits of threads and processes.
- The asynchronous programming paradigm is preferred or required.

Non-Blocking I/O is Required

Asyncio is specifically designed for non-blocking I/O with subprocesses and TCP socket connections.

If an application requires a large number of concurrent socket or subprocess tasks then asyncio is an obvious choice.

Poster-child examples include:

- Executing and checking the results of many commands on a system.
- Making and managing many socket connections.
- Serving access to many client socket connections.

Although this is the focus of the `asyncio` module, it is not the only reason to adopt it in a project.

Coroutine-Based Concurrency is Required

Coroutines and asyncio offer an alternative to concurrency with threads or processes.

Each of threads, processes, and coroutines have benefits and limitations. Coroutines and the `asyncio` module together provide an alternative to concurrent programming.

Generally, coroutines are lightweight, they are just a type of function. The use less memory and are faster to start, suspend, and resume than threads and processes that are managed by the underlying operating system.

An asyncio program may have orders of magnitude more concurrent coroutines than a threading program can have concurrent threads or a multiprocessing program can have concurrent processes.

Asyncio be may required if a program may have tens or hundreds of thousands of concurrent tasks.

Asynchronous Programming is Required

Asynchronous programming is a new or modern type of programming.

It has proven very popular in other programming languages, such as JavaScript.

Coroutines and asyncio unlock this capability in the Python interpreter and standard library, with no third-party libraries needed.

Adopting asyncio for a project may be appropriate if the asynchronous programming paradigm is preferred. Sometimes a programming paradigm is chosen beforehand, making it a de facto requirement.

Asynchronous programming with asyncio could be used instead of or in complement to a procedural-programming, object-oriented programming or functional programming paradigm.

When Not to Use Asyncio

Asyncio should not always be used.

Python provides robust and capable thread-based concurrency and process-based concurrency. These options should be used in most cases for concurrent programming in Python for I/O-bound tasks and CPU-bound tasks respectively.

Modern thread pools in the `concurrent.futures` module support asynchronous ad hoc tasks using both threads and processes. This provides an alternative way of adding elements of asynchronous programming, without adopting coroutines.

A mistake is to think that asyncio is going to make the program faster than thread or processes, or that coroutines cannot suffer race conditions or deadlocks. Both of these notions are false.

Downloading webpages or querying open ports is just as fast with concurrent threads as concurrent coroutines in one thread.

Code must be made coroutine-safe when using coroutine-based concurrency, just like it must be made thread-safe when using threads and process-safe when using process-based concurrency. There is no escape from these concepts when using concurrent programming.

Another mistake is to think that asyncio makes concurrent programming easy.

Concurrent programming is always hard, regardless of the unit of concurrency or programming paradigm.

Coroutines can make code easier to read. The coroutine definitions look and read like functions. But the challenges of good design and safety in concurrent programming do not go just by changing the unit of concurrency, we described previously.

In fact, the adoption of asynchronous programming may introduce new and different challenges.

Lesson Review

Takeaways

Well done, you made it to the end of the lesson.

- You now know what is a coroutine and how it relates to routines, threads, and generators.
- You now know what is asynchronous programming and asynchronous I/O.
- You now know what the `asyncio` module is in Python and the capabilities it provides.
- You now know how to develop a hello world asyncio program and know how it works.
- You now know when to use asyncio in your Python programs.

Exercise

Your task for this lesson is to take what you have learned about asyncio and think about where you could use it to improve the performance of your programs.

List at least three examples of programs you have worked on recently that could benefit from the concurrency provided by coroutines and the `asyncio` module. No need to share sensitive details of the project or technical details on how exactly asyncio could be used, just a one or two line high-level description is sufficient.

If you have trouble coming up with examples of recent applications that may benefit from using asyncio, then think of applications or functionality you could develop for current or future projects that could make good use of asynchronous programming.

This is a useful exercise, as it will start to train your brain to see when you can and cannot make use of these techniques in practice.

Share your results online on Twitter, LinkedIn, GitHub, or similar.

Send me the link to your results, I'd love to see what you come up with.

You can send me a message directly via:

- Super Fast Python - Contact Page
  https://SuperFastPython.com/contact/

Or share it with me on Twitter via @SuperFastPython.

Further Reading

This section provides resources for you to learn more about the topics covered in this lesson.

- `asyncio` - Asynchronous I/O.
  https://docs.python.org/3/library/asyncio.html
- PEP 492 - Coroutines with async and await syntax.
  https://peps.python.org/pep-0492/
- PEP 3156 - Asynchronous IO Support Rebooted: the `asyncio` Module.
  https://peps.python.org/pep-3156/
- Asynchronous I/O, Wikipedia.
  https://en.wikipedia.org/wiki/Asynchronous_I/O
- Async/await, Wikipedia.
  https://en.wikipedia.org/wiki/Async/await
- Coroutine, Wikipedia.
  https://en.wikipedia.org/wiki/Coroutine
- Cooperative multitasking, Wikipedia.
  https://en.wikipedia.org/wiki/Cooperative_multitasking

Next

In the next lesson, we will explore more about how to define coroutines and how to create, schedule and query asynchronous tasks.

Lesson 02: Coroutines and Tasks

In this lesson, we will explore how to create and use coroutines and tasks in asyncio programs. These are the primary units of concurrency in asyncio programs that can be suspended, resumed, canceled and more.

After completing this lesson, you will know:

- How to define, create, and run a coroutine with the `async` and `await` expressions.
- How to create and schedule a coroutine as an independent task.
- How to query the status of asyncio tasks, get results, and check for exceptions.
- How to cancel asyncio tasks and add done callback functions.

Let's get started.

How to Create and Run Coroutines

A coroutine is a function that can be suspended and resumed.

Python provides coroutines for concurrency.

They are provided in two main ways:

- Through specific additions to the language, e.g. `async` and `await` expressions.

- Through a specific module in the standard library, e.g. `asyncio` module.

Let's explore how we can create and use coroutines.

How to Define a Coroutine

A coroutine can be defined via the `async def` expression.

This is an extension of the `def` expression for defining subroutines.

It defines a coroutine that can be created and returns a coroutine object.

For example:

```
# define a coroutine
async def custom_coro():
    # ...
```

A coroutine defined with the `async def` expression is referred to as a *coroutine function*.

A coroutine function can take arguments and return a value, just like a regular function.

Another key difference is that it can use special coroutine expressions, such as `await`, `async for`, and `async with`.

We will look at the `await` expression soon in a following section. We will learn about the `async for`, and `async with` expressions in *Lesson 04: Iterators, Generators, and Context Managers*.

Next, let's look at how to create a coroutine.

How to Create a Coroutine

Once a coroutine is defined, it can be created.

This looks like calling a subroutine.

For example:

```
...
# create a coroutine
coro = custom_coro()
```

This does not execute the coroutine.

It returns a `coroutine` object.

A `coroutine` object has methods, such as `send()` and `close()`. It is a type.

We can demonstrate this by creating an instance of a coroutine and calling the `type()` built-in function in order to report its type.

For example:

```
# SuperFastPython.com
# example of checking the type of a coroutine

# define a coroutine
async def custom_coro():
    # do nothing
    pass

# create the coroutine
coro = custom_coro()
# check the type of the coroutine
print(type(coro))
```

Running the example reports that the created coroutine is a `coroutine` class.

A coroutine object is an awaitable.

This means it is a type that implements the `__await__()` method.

We also get a `RuntimeError` because the coroutine was created but never executed, we will explore that in the next section.

```
<class 'coroutine'>
sys:1: RuntimeWarning: coroutine '...' was never awaited
```

Next, let's look at how to run a coroutine.

How to Run a Coroutine

Coroutines can be defined and created, but they can only be executed within an event loop.

The event loop that executes coroutines, manages the cooperative multitasking between coroutines.

The typical way to start a coroutine event loop is via the `asyncio.run()` function.

This function takes one coroutine and returns the value of the coroutine. The provided coroutine can be used as the entry point into the coroutine-based program.

For example:

```
...
# create the coroutine
coro = custom_coroutine()
# start the event loop and execute the coroutine
asyncio.run(coro)
```

This approach to executing a coroutine is typically performed in a single line.

For example:

```
...
# start the event loop and execute the coroutine
asyncio.run(custom_coroutine())
```

This will start the asyncio runtime, called the event loop, and execute the coroutine.

It is the primary way that asyncio applications are started.

For example:

```
# SuperFastPython.com
# example of running a coroutine
```

```python
import asyncio

# main coroutine
async def main():
    # report a message
    print('Hello from a coroutine')

# start the coroutine program
asyncio.run(main())
```

Running the example creates the `main()` coroutine and passes the coroutine object to the `run()` function.

The `run()` function then starts the asyncio event loop and schedules the `main()` coroutine.

The `main()` coroutine executes and reports a message.

The coroutine terminates. There are no further coroutines to execute, so the event loop terminates.

```
Hello from a coroutine
```

Next, let's look at how to await a coroutine.

How to Await a Coroutine

Another way to run a coroutine is to await it from a running coroutine.

This requires the use of the `await` expression.

The `await` expression takes an awaitable and suspends the caller. It schedules the provided awaitable if needed. The caller will resume only once the provided awaitable is done.

For example:

```python
...
# await an awaitable
await coro
```

An awaitable is an object that can be waited on using the `await` expression.

It is an object that implements the __await__() method.

Coroutines are awaitables, but so too are `asyncio.Task` and `asyncio.Future` objects.

We can execute a coroutine by awaiting it directly from within another coroutine.

For example:

```
# defines a custom coroutine
async def another_coroutine():
    ...
    # create the coroutine
    coro = custom_coroutine()
    # execute and wait for the coroutine to finish
    await coro
```

This is typically performed in a single line.

For example:

```
...
# execute and wait for the coroutine to finish
await custom_coroutine()
```

The `asyncio` API provides coroutine functions that return coroutine objects that can be awaited.

An example is `asyncio.sleep()`. This function takes a number of seconds as an integer or floating point value and returns a coroutine that can be awaited.

For example:

```
...
# execute and wait for the coroutine to finish
await asyncio.sleep(1)
```

This suspends the caller and executes a coroutine that sleeps for a given number of seconds, e.g. is also suspended.

It is a helpful function that we will use often to simulate a coroutine doing some work.

The example below executes a coroutine that in turn executes and awaits the `asyncio.sleep()` coroutine.

```python
# SuperFastPython.com
# example of running a coroutine from a coroutine
import asyncio

# main coroutine
async def main():
    # report a message
    print('Hello from a coroutine')
    # sleep for a moment
    await asyncio.sleep(1)

# start the coroutine program
asyncio.run(main())
```

Running the example creates the `main()` coroutine and passes the coroutine object to the `run()` function.

The `run()` function then starts the asyncio event loop and schedules the `main()` coroutine.

The `main()` coroutine executes and reports a message. It then creates the `sleep()` coroutine and schedules it for execution, suspending it until it is done.

The `sleep()` coroutine runs and suspends itself for a fixed number of seconds.

The `sleep()` coroutine terminates, then the `main()` coroutine resumes and terminates.

There are no further coroutines to execute, so the event loop terminates.

```
Hello from a coroutine
```

We now know how to create and run coroutines in asyncio programs.

Next, let's explore asyncio tasks.

How to Create and Run Tasks

Asyncio provides tasks that provide a way to wrap and execute coroutines independently.

The benefit is that the task provides a handle on the coroutine that can be queried, from which results can be retrieved, and provides a way to cancel a running coroutine.

In this section, we will explore how to create and run tasks in asyncio programs.

What is an Asyncio Task

An `asyncio.Task` is an object that schedules and independently runs an asyncio coroutine.

It provides a handle on a scheduled coroutine that an asyncio program can query and use to interact with the coroutine.

A task is created from a coroutine. It requires a coroutine object, wraps the coroutine, schedules it for execution, and provides ways to interact with it.

A task is executed independently. This means it is scheduled in the asyncio event loop and will execute regardless of what else happens in the coroutine that created it. This is different from executing a coroutine directly, where the caller must wait for it to complete.

The `asyncio.Task` class extends the `asyncio.Future` class and an instance are awaitable.

A `Future` is a lower-level class that represents a result that will eventually arrive.

Classes that extend the `Future` class are often referred to as **Future-like**.

Because a `Task` is awaitable it means that a coroutine can wait for a task to be done using the `await` expression.

For example:

```
...
# wait for a task to be done
await task
```

Now that we know what an asyncio task is, let's look at how we can create one.

How to Create a Task

A task is created using a provided coroutine instance.

In fact, a task can only be created and scheduled within a coroutine.

A task can be created using the `asyncio.create_task()` function.

The `asyncio.create_task()` function takes a coroutine instance and an optional name for the task and returns an `asyncio.Task` instance.

For example:

```
...
# create a coroutine
coro = task_coroutine()
# create a task from a coroutine
task = asyncio.create_task(coro)
```

This can be achieved with a compound statement on a single line.

For example:

```
...
# create a task from a coroutine
task = asyncio.create_task(task_coroutine())
```

This will do a few things:

1. Wrap the coroutine in a `Task` instance.
2. Schedule the task for execution in the event loop.

3. Return a `Task` instance

The task instance can be discarded, interacted with via methods, and awaited by a coroutine.

There are other ways to create a task using the low-level API, but this is the preferred way to create a `Task` from a coroutine in an asyncio program.

Next, let's look at when exactly the task will run.

When Does the Task Run

A common question after creating a task is when does it run?

This is a good question.

Although we can schedule a coroutine to run independently as a task with the `create_task()` function, it may not run immediately.

In fact, the task will not execute until the event loop has an opportunity to execute it.

This will not happen until all other coroutines are not running and it is the task's turn to run.

For example, if we had an asyncio program with one coroutine that created and scheduled a task, the scheduled task will not run until the calling coroutine that created the task is suspended.

This may happen if the calling coroutine chooses to sleep, chooses to await another coroutine or task, or chooses to await the new task that was scheduled.

For example:

```
...
# create a task from a coroutine
task = asyncio.create_task(task_coroutine())
# await the task, allowing it to run
await task
```

Now that we know what a task is and how to create one, let's look at a worked example.

Example of Creating and Running a Task

We can explore an example of creating a Task from a coroutine in an asyncio program.

This is the quintessential use case of creating and using a task.

In this example, we will define a coroutine that we will wrap in a task. We will then define the main coroutine that will be the entry point of the program. A task will be created from our task coroutine and then await the task to complete.

The complete example is listed below.

```python
# SuperFastPython.com
# example of creating and awaiting an asyncio task
import asyncio

# define a coroutine for a task
async def task_coroutine():
    # report a message
    print('executing the task')
    # suspend for a moment
    await asyncio.sleep(1)

# custom coroutine
async def main():
    # report a message
    print('main coroutine')
    # create and schedule the task
    task = asyncio.create_task(task_coroutine())
    # wait for the task to complete
    await task

# start the asyncio program
asyncio.run(main())
```

Running the example first creates the `main()` coroutine and uses it as the entry point to the asyncio program.

The `main()` coroutine then reports a message. It then creates an instance of the `task_coroutine()` coroutine and passes it to the `create_task()` function in order to wrap it in a `Task` instance and return the instance.

This schedules the `Task`-wrapped coroutine for execution as soon as it is able.

The `main()` coroutine then continues on and then suspends execution and awaits the task to be completed.

This gives the task an opportunity to execute. It reports a message and then suspends, sleeping for one second.

At this time both the `main()` coroutine and the `Task` are suspended.

The `Task` resumes and then terminates.

The `main()` coroutine then continues on and terminates, which closes the asyncio program.

```
main coroutine
executing the task
```

Now that we know how to create tasks, let's look at how we can interact with them.

How to Use Asyncio Tasks

The `asyncio.Task` object provides a handle on a scheduled coroutine.

It provides a number of methods that we can use in our asyncio programs to query and interact with the coroutine.

In this section, we will explore how to use `asyncio.Task` objects once they have been created.

How to Check Task Status

After a `Task` is created we can check its status.

There are two statuses we can check, they are:

- Whether the task is done.
- Whether the task was canceled.

Let's take a closer look at each in turn.

Check if a Task is Done

We can check if a task is done via the `done()` method.

The method returns `True` if the task is done, or `False` otherwise.

For example:

```
...
# check if a task is done
if task.done():
    # ...
```

A task is done if it has had the opportunity to run and is now no longer running.

A task that has been scheduled is not done. Similarly, a task that is running is not done.

A task is done if:

- The coroutine finishes normally.
- The coroutine returns explicitly.
- An unexpected error or exception is raised in the coroutine
- The task is canceled.

Check if a Task is Canceled

We can check if a task is canceled via the `cancelled()` method.

The method returns `True` if the task was canceled, or `False` otherwise.

For example:

```
...
# check if a task was canceled
if task.cancelled():
    # ...
```

A task is canceled if the `cancel()` method was called on the task and completed successfully, e..g `cancel()` returned `True`.

A task is not canceled if the `cancel()` method was not called, or if the `cancel()` method was called but failed to cancel the task.

Next, let's look at how we can get the result from a task.

How to Get a Tasks Result

We can get the return value from the coroutine wrapped by the task by simply awaiting the task.

For example:

```
...
# get the return value from the wrapped coroutine
value = await task
```

Another approach to get the result of a task via the `result()` method.

This returns the return value of the coroutine wrapped by the `Task` or `None` if the wrapped coroutine does not explicitly return a value.

For example:

```
...
# get the return value from the wrapped coroutine
value = task.result()
```

If the coroutine raises an unhandled error or exception, it is re-raised when calling the `result()` method and may need to be handled.

For example:

```
...
try:
    # get the return value from the wrapped coroutine
    value = task.result()
except Exception:
    # task failed and there is no result
```

If the task was canceled, then a `CancelledError` exception is raised when calling the `result()` method and may need to be handled.

For example:

```
...
try:
    # get the return value from the wrapped coroutine
    value = task.result()
except asyncio.CancelledError:
    # task was canceled
```

As such, it is a good idea to check if the task was canceled first.

For example:

```
...
# check if the task was not canceled
if not task.cancelled():
    # get the return value from the wrapped coroutine
    value = task.result()
else:
    # task was canceled
```

If the task is not yet done, then an `InvalidStateError` exception is raised when calling the `result()` method and may need to be handled.

For example:

```
...
try:
    # get the return value from the wrapped coroutine
    value = task.result()
except asyncio.InvalidStateError:
```

```
# task is not yet done
```

As such, it is a good idea to check if the task is done first.

For example:

```
...
# check if the task is not done
if not task.done():
    await task
# get the return value from the wrapped coroutine
value = task.result()
```

Next, let's look at how we can get an unhandled exception raised by a task.

How to Get a Tasks Exception

A coroutine wrapped by a task may raise an exception that is not handled.

This will cause the task to *fail*, in effect.

We can retrieve an unhandled exception in the coroutine wrapped by a task via the `exception()` method.

For example:

```
...
# get the exception raised by a task
exception = task.exception()
```

If an unhandled exception was not raised in the wrapped coroutine, then a value of `None` is returned.

If the task was canceled, then a `CancelledError` exception is raised when calling the `exception()` method and may need to be handled.

Similarly, if the task is not yet done, then an `InvalidStateError` exception is raised when calling the `exception()` method and may need to be handled.

Next, let's look at how we can cancel a running task.

How to Cancel a Task

We can cancel a scheduled task via the `cancel()` method.

The cancel method returns **True** if the task was canceled, or **False** otherwise.

For example:

```
...
# cancel the task
was_cancelled = task.cancel()
```

If the task is already done, it cannot be canceled and the `cancel()` method will return **False** and the task will not have the status of canceled.

If cancel request was successfully, the next time the task is given an opportunity to run, it will raise a `CancelledError` exception.

If the `CancelledError` exception is not handled within the wrapped coroutine, the task will be canceled.

Otherwise, if the `CancelledError` exception is handled within the wrapped coroutine, the task will not be canceled.

The `cancel()` method can also take a message argument which will be used in the content of the `CancelledError`.

We can explore how to cancel a task.

In this example, we will create and schedule a task as per normal. The caller will then wait a moment and allow the task to begin executing.

It will then cancel the task and check that the request to cancel was successful.

The caller will then wait a moment more for the task to be canceled, then report the status of the task to confirm it is marked as canceled.

The complete example is listed below.

```python
# SuperFastPython.com
# example of canceling an asyncio task
import asyncio

# define a coroutine for a task
async def task_coroutine():
    # report a message
    print('executing the task')
    # suspend for a moment
    await asyncio.sleep(1)

# custom coroutine
async def main():
    # report a message
    print('main coroutine')
    # create and schedule the task
    task = asyncio.create_task(task_coroutine())
    # wait a moment
    await asyncio.sleep(0.5)
    # cancel the task
    was_cancelled = task.cancel()
    print(f'>was canceled: {was_cancelled}')
    # wait a moment
    await asyncio.sleep(0.1)
    # report the status
    print(f'>canceled: {task.cancelled()}')

# start the asyncio program
asyncio.run(main())
```

Running the example first creates the main() coroutine and uses it as the entry point to the asyncio program.

The main() coroutine then reports a message. It then creates an instance of the task_coroutine() coroutine and passes it to the create_task() method in order to wrap it in a Task instance and return the instance.

The **main()** coroutine then suspends execution and suspends for half a second.

This gives the task an opportunity to execute the task. The task reports a message and then suspends, sleeping for one second.

The **main()** coroutine resumes and cancels the new task. It then reports whether the request to cancel the task was successful. It was because we know that the task is not yet done. The **main()** coroutine then suspends for a fraction of a second.

This gives the task another opportunity to execute, in which case the **CancelledError** exception is raised in the wrapped coroutine, canceling the task.

The **main()** coroutine then resumes and checks the canceled status of the task, confirming that it indeed is done and was canceled.

```
main coroutine
executing the task
>was canceled: True
>canceled: True
```

Next, let's look at how we can add a done callback function to a task.

How to Use Callback With a Task

We can add a done callback function to a task via the **add_done_callback()** method.

This method takes the name of a function to call when the task is done.

The callback function must take the **Task** instance as an argument.

For example:

```
# done callback function
def handle(task):
    print(task)
```

```
...
# register a done callback function
task.add_done_callback(handle)
```

Recall that a task may be done when the wrapped coroutine finishes normally when it returns, when an unhandled exception is raised or when the task is canceled.

The add_done_callback() method can be used to add or register as many done callback functions as we like.

We can also remove or de-register a callback function via the remove_done_callback() function.

For example:

```
...
# remove a done callback function
task.remove_done_callback(handle)
```

We can explore how to use a done callback function on a task.

In this example, we will define a done callback function that will report whether a task is done or not.

The function will then be registered on the task after it is created.

The complete example is listed below.

```
# SuperFastPython.com
# example of adding a done callback function to a task
import asyncio

# custom done callback function
def handle(task):
    print(f'Task callback done: {task.done()}')

# define a coroutine for a task
async def task_coroutine():
    # report a message
    print('executing the task')
    # suspend for a moment
```

```
    await asyncio.sleep(1)

# custom coroutine
async def main():
    # report a message
    print('main coroutine')
    # create and schedule the task
    task = asyncio.create_task(task_coroutine())
    # add a done callback function
    task.add_done_callback(handle)
    # wait for the task to complete
    await task

# start the asyncio program
asyncio.run(main())
```

Running the example first creates the **main()** coroutine and uses it as the entry point to the asyncio program.

The **main()** coroutine then reports a message. It then creates an instance of the **task_coroutine()** coroutine and passes it to the **create_task()** method in order to wrap it in a **Task** instance and return the instance.

The **main()** coroutine then registers the done callback function on the task. It then suspends execution and awaits the task to be completed.

This gives the task an opportunity to execute. It reports a message and then suspends, sleeping for one second. It resumes and terminates.

This triggers the asyncio infrastructure to call the callback function and pass it the **Task** instance.

The callback function is executed and reports a message, confirming that indeed the task is marked as done.

```
main coroutine
executing the task
Task callback done: True
```

Next, let's look at how we can assign a meaningful name to a task.

How to Set the Task Name

A task may have a name.

This name can be helpful if multiple tasks are created from the same coroutine and we need some way to tell them apart programmatically.

The name can be set when the task is created from a coroutine via the **name** argument.

For example:

```
...
# create a coroutine
coro = task_coroutine()
# create a task from a coroutine
task = asyncio.create_task(coro, name='MyTask')
```

The name for the task can also be set via the **set_name()** method.

For example:

```
...
# set the name of the task
task.set_name('MyTask')
```

We can retrieve the name of a task via the **get_name()** method.

For example:

```
...
# get the name of a task
name = task.get_name()
```

This is just a sample of some of the key ways that we can interact with an `asyncio.Task` that represents a scheduled coroutine.

Lesson Review

Takeaways

Well done, you made it to the end of the lesson.

- You now know how to define, create, and run a coroutine with the `async` and `await` expressions.
- You now know how to create and schedule a coroutine as an independent task.
- You now know how to query the status of asyncio tasks, get results, and check for exceptions.
- You now know how to cancel asyncio tasks and add done callback functions.

Exercise

Your task for this lesson is to use what you have just learned about running ad hoc code in a coroutine or independent task.

Devise a small asyncio program that executes a repetitive task, such as calling the same function multiple times in a loop. Execute this program and record how long it takes to complete.

The specifics of the task do not matter. You can try to complete something practical, or if you run out of ideas, you can calculate a number, or suspend with the `asyncio.sleep()` function.

Now update the program to execute each task using a separate coroutines executed concurrently as independent `asyncio.Tasks`. Record how long it takes to execute.

Compare the execution time between the serial and concurrent versions of the program. Calculate the difference in seconds (e.g. it is faster by 5 seconds). Calculate the ratio that the second program is faster than the first program (e.g. it is 2.5x faster).

These calculations may help:

- difference $= serial\_time - concurrent\_time$
- ratio $= \frac{serial\_time}{concurrent\_time}$

If it turns out that the asynchronous version of the program is not faster, perhaps change or manipulate the task so that the serial version is slower than the faster version.

This exercise will help you develop the calculations and practice needed to benchmark and compare the performance before and after making code concurrent with asyncio.

Share your results online on Twitter, LinkedIn, GitHub, or similar.

Send me the link to your results, I'd love to see what you come up with.

You can send me a message directly via:

- Super Fast Python - Contact Page
  https://SuperFastPython.com/contact/

Or share it with me on Twitter via @SuperFastPython.

Further Reading

This section provides resources for you to learn more about the topics covered in this lesson.

- `asyncio` - Asynchronous I/O.
  https://docs.python.org/3/library/asyncio.html
- PEP 492 - Coroutines with async and await syntax.
  https://peps.python.org/pep-0492/
- PEP 3156 - Asynchronous IO Support Rebooted: the `asyncio` Module.
  https://peps.python.org/pep-3156/
- Coroutines and Tasks.
  https://docs.python.org/3/library/asyncio-task.html
- Coroutine, Wikipedia.
  https://en.wikipedia.org/wiki/Coroutine

Next

In the next lesson, we will explore how to run multiple coroutines as a group and wait for groups of coroutines to complete or meet a condition.

Lesson 03: Collections of Tasks

In this lesson, we will explore how to run and work with collections of coroutines and asyncio tasks. This is the main way to issue and wait on many asynchronously issued and concurrently executing tasks at points in our program.

After completing this lesson, you will know:

- How to run many coroutines concurrently as a group and retrieve their results.
- How to wait for a collection of tasks to complete or for the first of a group to complete or fail.
- How to wait for an asynchronous task to complete with a timeout.
- How to handle task results in the order that tasks are completed.
- How to run blocking function calls asynchronously in a separate thread.

Let's get started.

How to Run Many Tasks as a Group

The `asyncio.gather()` function allows the caller to group multiple awaitables together and have them executed concurrently.

We may use the `asyncio.gather()` function in situations where we create many tasks or coroutines up-front and then wish to execute them all at once and wait for them all to complete before continuing on.

This is a likely situation where the result is required from many similar tasks, e.g. same task or coroutine with different data.

The awaitables can be executed concurrently, results returned, and the main program can resume by making use of the results.

Now that we know what the `asyncio.gather()` function is, let's look at how we can use it.

How to use `asyncio.gather()`

The `asyncio.gather()` function takes one or more awaitables as arguments.

Recall an awaitable may be a coroutine, a **Future** or a **Task**. Therefore, we can call the `gather()` function with multiple tasks, multiple coroutines, or a mixture of tasks and coroutines.

For example:

```
...
# execute multiple coroutines
asyncio.gather(coro1(), coro2())
```

If **Task** objects are provided to `gather()`, they will already be running because tasks are scheduled as part of being created.

The `asyncio.gather()` function takes awaitables as position arguments.

We cannot create a list or collection of awaitables and provide it to gather, as this will result in an error.

For example:

```
...
# create a list of coroutines
coros = [coro1(), coro2()]
```

```
# cannot provide a list of awaitables directly
asyncio.gather(corors) # error
```

A list of awaitables can be provided if it is first unpacked into separate expressions using the star operator (∗), also called the asterisk operator.

This operator specifically unpacks iterables, like lists, into separate expressions. It is often referred to as the iterable unpacking operator.

For example:

```
...
# create a list of coroutines
coros = [coro1(), coro2()]
# gather with an unpacked list of awaitables
asyncio.gather(*coros)
```

If coroutines are provided to `gather()`, they are wrapped in `Task` objects automatically.

The `gather()` function does not suspend directly. Instead, it returns an `asyncio.Future` object that represents the group of awaitables.

For example:

```
...
# get a future that represents multiple awaitables
group = asyncio.gather(coro1(), coro2())
```

Once the `Future` object is created it is scheduled automatically within the event loop.

This means that if the caller did nothing else, the scheduled group of awaitables will run (assuming the caller suspends). We can interact with the group via the `Future` object just like a task, such as add a done callback function, cancel the group and check on the status of the group.

Nevertheless, the most common usage of `asyncio.gather()` is to await the returned `Future` directly.

This will collect the return values from the coroutines and tasks and return them as an iterable.

For example:

```
...
# execute coroutines and get the return values
values = await asyncio.gather(coro1(), coro2())
```

Now that we know how to use `asyncio.gather()`, let's look at a worked example.

Example of Running Many Coroutines in a List

It is common to create multiple coroutines beforehand and then gather them later.

This allows a program to prepare the tasks that are to be executed concurrently and then trigger their concurrent execution all at once and wait for them to complete.

We can collect many coroutines together into a list either manually or using a list comprehension.

For example:

```
...
# create many coroutines
coros = [task_coro(i) for i in range(10)]
```

We can then call `gather()` with all coroutines in the list.

The list of coroutines cannot be provided directly to the `gather()` function as this will result in an error.

Instead, the `gather()` function requires each awaitable to be provided as a separate positional argument.

This can be achieved by unwrapping the list into separate expressions and passing them to the `gather()` function. The star operator (*) will perform this operation for us.

For example:

```
...
# run the tasks
await asyncio.gather(*coros)
```

Tying this together, the complete example of running a list of pre-prepared coroutines with **gather()** is listed below.

```
# SuperFastPython.com
# example of gather for many coroutines in a list
import asyncio

# coroutine used for a task
async def task_coro(value):
    # report a message
    print(f'>task {value} executing')
    # sleep for a moment
    await asyncio.sleep(1)

# coroutine used for the entry point
async def main():
    # report a message
    print('main starting')
    # create many coroutines
    coros = [task_coro(i) for i in range(10)]
    # run the tasks
    await asyncio.gather(*coros)
    # report a message
    print('main done')

# start the asyncio program
asyncio.run(main())
```

Running the example executes the **main()** coroutine as the entry point to the program.

The **main()** coroutine then creates a list of 10 coroutine objects using a list comprehension.

This list is then provided to the **gather()** function and unpacked into 10 separate expressions using the star operator.

The `main()` coroutine then awaits the `Future` object returned from the call to `gather()`, suspending and waiting for all scheduled coroutines to complete their execution.

The coroutines run as soon as they are able, reporting their unique messages and sleeping before terminating.

Only after all coroutines in the group are complete does the `main()` coroutine resume and report its final message.

This highlights how we can prepare a collection of coroutines and provide them as separate expressions to the `gather()` function.

```
main starting
>task 0 executing
>task 1 executing
>task 2 executing
>task 3 executing
>task 4 executing
>task 5 executing
>task 6 executing
>task 7 executing
>task 8 executing
>task 9 executing
main done
```

Next, let's look at how we can wait for many tasks in an asyncio program.

How to Wait for Many Tasks

The `asyncio.wait()` function can be used to wait for a collection of asyncio tasks to complete.

Recall that an asyncio task is an instance of the `asyncio.Task` class that wraps a coroutine. It allows a coroutine to be scheduled and executed independently, and the `Task` instance provides a handle on the task for querying status and getting results.

The `wait()` function allows us to wait for a collection of tasks to be done.

The call to wait can be configured to wait for different conditions, such as all tasks being completed, the first task completed and the first task failing with an error.

Next, let's look at how we can use the `wait()` function.

How to Use `asyncio.wait()`

The `asyncio.wait()` function takes a collection of awaitables, typically `Task` objects.

This could be a `list`, `dict`, or `set` of task objects that we have created, such as via calls to the `asyncio.create_task()` task function in a list comprehension.

For example:

```
...
# create many tasks
tsks = [asyncio.create_task(task(i)) for i in range(10)]
```

The `asyncio.wait()` will not return until some condition on the collection of tasks is met.

By default, the condition is that all tasks are completed.

The `wait()` function returns a tuple of two sets. The first set contains all task objects that meet the condition, and the second contains all other task objects that do not yet meet the condition.

These sets are referred to as the *done* set and the *pending* set.

For example:

```
...
# wait for all tasks to complete
done, pending = await asyncio.wait(tasks)
```

Technically, the `asyncio.wait()` is a coroutine function that returns a coroutine.

We can then await this coroutine which will return the tuple of sets.

For example:

```
...
# create the wait coroutine
wait_coro = asyncio.wait(tasks)
# await the wait coroutine
t = await wait_coro
```

The condition waited for can be specified by the `return_when` argument which is set to `asyncio.ALL_COMPLETED` by default.

For example:

```
...
# wait for all tasks to complete
done, pending = await asyncio.wait(tasks,
    return_when=asyncio.ALL_COMPLETED)
```

We can wait for the first task to be completed by setting `return_when` to `FIRST_COMPLETED`.

For example:

```
...
# wait for the first task to be completed
done, pending = await asyncio.wait(tasks,
    return_when=asyncio.FIRST_COMPLETED)
```

When the first task is complete and returned in the done set, the remaining tasks are not canceled and continue to execute concurrently.

We can wait for the first task to fail with an exception by setting `return_when` to `FIRST_EXCEPTION`.

For example:

```
...
# wait for the first task to fail
done, pending = await asyncio.wait(tasks,
    return_when=asyncio.FIRST_EXCEPTION)
```

In this case, the done set will contain the first task that failed with an exception. If no task fails with an exception, the done set will contain all tasks and `wait()` will return only after all tasks are completed.

We can specify how long we are willing to wait for the given condition via a `timeout` argument in seconds.

If the timeout expires before the condition is met, the tuple of tasks is returned with whatever subset of tasks do meet the condition at that time, e.g. the subset of tasks that are completed if waiting for all tasks to complete.

For example:

```
...
# wait for all tasks to complete with a timeout
done, pending = await asyncio.wait(tasks, timeout=3)
```

If the timeout is reached before the condition is met, an exception is not raised and the remaining tasks are not canceled.

Now that we know how to use the `asyncio.wait()` function, let's look at a worked example.

Example of Waiting for All Tasks

We can explore how to wait for all tasks using `asyncio.wait()`.

In this example, we will define a simple task coroutine that generates a random value, sleeps for a fraction of a second, then reports a message with the generated value.

The main coroutine will then create many tasks in a list comprehension with the coroutine and then wait for all tasks to be complete.

The complete example is listed below.

```
# SuperFastPython.com
# example of waiting for all tasks to complete
from random import random
import asyncio

# coroutine to execute in a new task
```

```python
async def task_coro(arg):
    # generate a random value between 0 and 1
    value = random()
    # suspend for a moment
    await asyncio.sleep(value)
    # report the value
    print(f'>task {arg} done with {value}')

# main coroutine
async def main():
    # create many tasks
    tasks = [asyncio.create_task(task_coro(i))
        for i in range(10)]
    # wait for all tasks to complete
    _ = await asyncio.wait(tasks)
    # report results
    print('All done')

# start the asyncio program
asyncio.run(main())
```

Running the example first creates the main() coroutine and uses it as the entry point into the asyncio program.

The main() coroutine then creates a list of ten tasks in a list comprehension, each providing a unique integer argument from 0 to 9.

The main() coroutine is then suspended and waits for all tasks to complete.

The tasks execute. Each generates a random value, sleeps for a moment, then reports its generated value.

After all tasks have been completed, the main() coroutine resumes and reports a final message.

This example highlights how we can use the wait() function to wait for a collection of tasks to be completed.

This is perhaps the most common usage of the function.

NOTE: Results will vary each time the program is run given the use of random numbers.

```
>task 5 done with 0.0591009105682192
>task 8 done with 0.10453715687017351
>task 0 done with 0.15462838864295925
>task 6 done with 0.4103492027393125
>task 9 done with 0.45567100006991623
>task 2 done with 0.6984682905809402
>task 7 done with 0.7785363531316224
>task 3 done with 0.827386088873161
>task 4 done with 0.9481344994700972
>task 1 done with 0.9577302665040541
All done
```

Next, let's look at how we can wait for a coroutine to complete with a fixed timeout.

How to Wait For a Task With a Timeout

The `asyncio.wait_for()` function allows the caller to wait for an asyncio task or coroutine to complete with a timeout.

If no timeout is specified, the `wait_for()` function will wait until the task is completed.

If a timeout is specified and elapses before the task is complete, then the task is canceled.

This allows the caller to both set an expectation about how long they are willing to wait for a task to complete, and to enforce the timeout by canceling the task if the timeout elapses.

Now that we know what the `asyncio.wait_for()` function is, let's look at how to use it.

How to Use `asyncio.wait_for()`

The `asyncio.wait_for()` function takes an awaitable and a timeout.

The awaitable may be a coroutine or a task.

A timeout must be specified and may be `None` for no timeout, an integer or floating point number of seconds.

The `wait_for()` function returns a coroutine that is not executed until it is explicitly awaited or scheduled as a task.

For example:

```
...
# wait for a task to complete
await asyncio.wait_for(coro, timeout=10)
```

If a coroutine is provided, it will be converted to the task when the `wait_for()` coroutine is executed.

If the timeout elapses before the task is completed, the task is canceled, and an `asyncio.TimeoutError` is raised, which may need to be handled.

For example:

```
...
# execute a task with a timeout
try:
    # wait for a task to complete
    await asyncio.wait_for(coro, timeout=1)
except asyncio.TimeoutError:
    # ...
```

If the waited-for task fails with an unhandled exception, the exception will be propagated back to the caller that is awaiting on the `wait_for()` coroutine, in which case it may need to be handled.

For example

```
...
# execute a task that may fail
try:
```

```
    # wait for a task to complete
    await asyncio.wait_for(coro, timeout=1)
except asyncio.TimeoutError:
    # ...
except Exception:
    # ...
```

Now that we know how the `wait_for()` function works, let's look at a worked example.

Example of Waiting for a Task with a Timeout

We can explore how to wait for a coroutine with a timeout that elapses before the task is completed.

In this example, we execute a coroutine except the caller waits a fixed timeout of 0.2 seconds or 200 milliseconds.

Recall that one second is equal to 1,000 milliseconds.

The task coroutine is modified so that it sleeps for more than one second, ensuring that the timeout always expires before the task is complete.

The complete example is listed below.

```
# SuperFastPython.com
# example of waiting for a coroutine with a timeout
from random import random
import asyncio

# coroutine to execute in a new task
async def task_coro():
    # generate a random value between 1 and 2
    value = 1 + random()
    # report message
    print(f'>task got {value}')
    # suspend for a moment
    await asyncio.sleep(value)
```

```
    # report all done
    print('>task done')

# main coroutine
async def main():
    # create a task
    task = task_coro()
    # execute and wait for the task without a timeout
    try:
        await asyncio.wait_for(task, timeout=0.2)
    except asyncio.TimeoutError:
        print('Gave up waiting, task canceled')

# start the asyncio program
asyncio.run(main())
```

Running the example first creates the `main()` coroutine and uses it as the entry point into the asyncio program.

The `main()` coroutine creates the task coroutine. It then calls `wait_for()` and passes the task coroutine and sets the timeout to 0.2 seconds.

The `main()` coroutine is suspended and the `task_coro()` is executed. It reports a message and sleeps for a moment.

The `main()` coroutine resumes after the timeout has elapsed. The `wait_for()` coroutine cancels the `task_coro()` coroutine and the `main()` coroutine is suspended.

The `task_coro()` runs again and responds to the request to be terminated. It raises a `TimeoutError` exception and terminates.

The `main()` coroutine resumes and handles the `TimeoutError` raised by the `task_coro()`.

This highlights how we can call the `wait_for()` function with a timeout and to cancel a task if it is not completed within a timeout.

NOTE: Results will vary each time the program is run given the use of random numbers.

```
>task got 1.4231068884240894
Gave up waiting, task canceled
```

Next, let's look at how we can handle coroutine results in the order they are completed.

How to Handle Tasks In Completion Order

The `asyncio.as_completed()` function will run a collection of tasks and coroutines concurrently.

More importantly, it returns an iterable that we can use to retrieve the awaitables in the order that they are completed.

It allows us to execute many coroutines or tasks concurrently and get the results from tasks as they are done, rather than the order we issued them.

Now that we know what `as_completed()` is, let's look at how we can use it.

How to Use `asyncio.as_completed()`

The `asyncio.as_completed()` function is called with a collection of awaitables.

This may be a list, dict, or set, and may contain `asyncio.Task` objects, coroutines, or other awaitables.

Any coroutines provided to `as_completed()` will be wrapped in a `Task` object for independent execution.

It returns an iterable that when traversed will yield awaitables in the provided list. These can be awaited by the caller in order to get results in the order that tasks are completed, e.g. get the result from the next task to complete.

For example:

```
...
# iterate over awaitables
for task in asyncio.as_completed(tasks):
    # get the next result
    result = await task
```

The `as_completed()` function also takes a `timeout` argument.

This specifies how long the caller is willing to wait for all awaitables to be done.

For example:

```
...
# iterate over awaitables with a timeout
for task in asyncio.as_completed(tasks, timeout=10):
    # get the next result
    result = await task
```

If the timeout elapses before all awaitables are done, a `asyncio.TimeoutError` is raised and may need to be handled.

For example, we could handle it within the loop:

```
...
# iterate over awaitables with a timeout
for task in asyncio.as_completed(tasks, timeout=10):
    # handle a timeout
    try:
        # get the next result
        result = await task
    except asyncio.TimeoutError:
        # ...
```

This is not desirable because once the timeout has elapsed, an `asyncio.TimeoutError` will be raised each time `next()` is called on the generator.

Therefore, it is better to wrap the entire loop in a try-except expression.

For example:

```
...
# handle a timeout
try:
    # iterate over awaitables with a timeout
    for task in asyncio.as_completed(tasks, timeout=10):
        # get the next result
        result = await task
except asyncio.TimeoutError:
    # ...
```

Now that we know how to use the `as_completed()` function, let's take a moment to consider how it works.

How Does `asyncio.as_completed()` Work

The function works by providing a generator that yields coroutines, where each coroutine will return a result of a provided awaitable.

The `asyncio.as_completed()` function does not suspend, but instead returns a generator.

For example:

```
...
# get a gen that yields awaitables in completion order
generator = asyncio.as_completed(tasks)
```

Calling the `next()` built-in function on the generator does not suspend, but instead yields a coroutine.

The returned coroutine is not one of the provided awaitables, but rather an internal coroutine from the `as_completed()` function that manages and monitors which issued task will return a result next.

For example:

```
...
# get the next coroutine
coro = next(generator)
```

It is not until one of the returned coroutines is awaited that the caller will suspend.

For example:

```
...
# get a result from the next task to complete
result = await coro
```

Now that we have an idea of how to use the as_completed() function and how it works, let's look at a worked example.

Example of Handling Task Results Dynamically

We can explore how to execute coroutines concurrently and get coroutine results as tasks are completed with the asyncio.as_completed() function.

In this example, we will define a simple coroutine task that takes an integer argument, generates a random value, sleeps for a fraction of a second then returns the integer argument multiplied by the generated value.

A list of the task coroutines is created and passed to the as_completed() function. This returns a generator that is traversed using a for-loop.

In each iteration of the loop a coroutine is yielded from the generator and is then awaited in the body of the loop. A result from the next coroutine to complete is returned and the result is reported.

The complete example is listed below.

```
# SuperFastPython.com
# example of getting coroutine results as completed
from random import random
import asyncio

# coroutine to execute in a new task
async def task_coro(arg):
    # generate a random value between 0 and 1
```

```python
    value = random()
    # suspend for a moment
    await asyncio.sleep(value)
    # return the result
    return arg * value

# main coroutine
async def main():
    # create many coroutines
    coros = [task_coro(i) for i in range(10)]
    # get results as coroutines are completed
    for coro in asyncio.as_completed(coros):
        # get the result from the next task to complete
        result = await coro
        # report the result
        print(f'>got {result}')

# start the asyncio program
asyncio.run(main())
```

Running the example first creates the `main()` coroutine and then uses this as the entry point into the asyncio program.

The `main()` coroutine runs and creates a list of coroutines.

It then passes this list to the `as_completed()` function which returns a generator. The generator is traversed in a for loop and each iteration yields a coroutine.

The coroutine is awaited. This suspends the `main()` coroutine.

The tasks begin executing, generating a random value, and sleeping. A task finishes and returns a value.

The `main()` coroutine resumes, receives the return value, and reports it.

The loop repeats, another coroutine is yielded, the `main()` coroutine awaits it and suspends, and another result is returned.

This continues until all coroutines in the provided list are completed.

This example highlights that we can traverse a collection of coroutines and get and use results in the order that tasks are completed.

NOTE: Results will vary each time the program is run given the use of random numbers.

```
>got 0.07236962530232949
>got 0.5171864910147306
>got 0.7153626682953872
>got 2.54812333824902
>got 0.5960648114598495
>got 5.051883987489034
>got 0.0
>got 2.842043340472799
>got 6.343694133393031
>got 4.903128525746293
```

Next, let's look at how we can call blocking functions without blocking the asyncio event loop.

How to Run Blocking Tasks

We can execute thread-blocking function calls in asyncio using the `asyncio.to_thread()` function.

It will take a function call and execute it in a new thread, separate from the thread that is executing the asyncio event loop.

It allows the asyncio event loop to treat a blocking function call as a coroutine and execute asynchronously using thread-based concurrency instead of coroutine-based concurrency.

The `asyncio.to_thread()` function is specifically designed to execute blocking I/O functions, not CPU-bound functions that can also block the asyncio event loop.

This is a useful function to use when we have an asyncio program that needs to perform both non-blocking I/O (such as with sockets) and blocking I/O (such as with files or a legacy API).

Now that we know how to execute blocking functions asynchronously in asyncio, let's look at how to use the `to_thread()` function.

How to Use `asyncio.to_thread()`

The `to_thread()` function takes the name of a blocking function to execute and any arguments to the function.

It then returns a coroutine that can be awaited to get the return value from the function, if any.

For example:

```
...
# create a coroutine for a blocking function
blocking_coro = asyncio.to_thread(blocking, arg1, arg2)
# await the coroutine and get return value
result = await blocking_coro
```

The blocking function will not be executed in a new thread until it is awaited or executed independently.

The coroutine can be wrapped in an `asyncio.Task` to execute the blocking function call independently.

For example:

```
...
# create a coroutine for a blocking function
blocking_coro = asyncio.to_thread(blocking)
# execute the blocking function independently
task = asyncio.create_task(blocking_coro)
```

This allows the blocking function call to be used like any other asyncio `Task`.

Now that we know how to use the `asyncio.to_thread()` function, let's look at a worked example.

Example of Running a Blocking Function in a Thread

We can explore how to execute the blocking call in a new thread and not stop the event loop.

In the example below we call `asyncio.to_thread()` to create a coroutine for the call to the `blocking_task()` function.

This coroutine is then awaited allowing the main coroutine to suspend and for the blocking function to execute in a new thread.

The complete example is listed below.

```python
# SuperFastPython.com
# example of running a blocking call in a new thread
import time
import asyncio

# blocking function
def blocking_task():
    # report a message
    print('task is running')
    # block the thread
    time.sleep(2)
    # report a message
    print('task is done')

# background coroutine task
async def background():
    # loop forever
    while True:
        # report a message
        print('>background task running')
        # sleep for a moment
        await asyncio.sleep(0.5)

# main coroutine
async def main():
```

```
    # run the background task
    _ = asyncio.create_task(background())
    # create a coroutine for the blocking function call
    coro = asyncio.to_thread(blocking_task)
    # make call in a new thread and await the result
    await coro

# start the asyncio program
asyncio.run(main())
```

Running the example first creates the `main()` coroutine and uses it as the entry point into the asyncio program.

The `main()` coroutine runs. It creates the background coroutine and schedules it for execution as soon as it can.

The `main()` coroutine then creates a coroutine to run the background task in a new thread and then awaits this coroutine.

This does a couple of things.

Firstly, it suspends the `main()` coroutine, allowing any other coroutines in the event loop to run, such as the new coroutine for executing the blocking function in a new thread.

The new coroutine runs and starts a new thread and executes the blocking function in the new thread. This coroutine was also suspended.

The event loop is free and the background coroutine gets an opportunity to run, looping and reporting its messages.

The blocking call in the other thread finishes, suspends the background task, resumes the main thread, and terminates the program.

This highlights that running a blocking call in a new thread does not block the event loop, allowing other coroutines to run while the blocking call is being executed, suspending some threads other than the main event loop thread.

```
task is running
>background task running
>background task running
>background task running
>background task running
task is done
```

Lesson Review

Takeaways

Well done, you made it to the end of the lesson.

- You now know how to run many coroutines concurrently as a group and retrieve their results.
- You now know how to wait for a collection of tasks to complete or for the first of a group to complete or fail.
- You now know how to wait for an asynchronous task to complete with a timeout.
- You now know how to handle task results in the order that tasks are completed.
- You now know how to run blocking function calls asynchronously in a separate thread.

Exercise

Your task for this lesson is to use what you have learned about running and waiting for many asynchronous tasks.

Develop a small asyncio program that creates and starts one or more asynchronous task performing some arbitrary activity, like sleeping.

Then from the main coroutine, wait for some time or a trigger and query the status one or more of the tasks you have created. For example, you could wait for all tasks to complete or for a timeout.

Extend the example so that the tasks take an random amount of time to complete or randomly raise an exception or not. Have the main coroutine wait for the first task to complete, the first to fail, or report results as they are completed.

This example will help you get used to working with and operating upon collections of asynchronous tasks that are executing concurrently.

Share your results online on Twitter, LinkedIn, GitHub, or similar.

Send me the link to your results, I'd love to see what you come up with.

You can send me a message directly via:

- Super Fast Python - Contact Page
  https://SuperFastPython.com/contact/

Or share it with me on Twitter via @SuperFastPython.

Further Reading

This section provides resources for you to learn more about the topics covered in this lesson.

- `asyncio` - Asynchronous I/O.
  https://docs.python.org/3/library/asyncio.html
- PEP 492 - Coroutines with async and await syntax.
  https://peps.python.org/pep-0492/
- PEP 3156 - Asynchronous IO Support Rebooted: the `asyncio` Module.
  https://peps.python.org/pep-3156/
- Coroutines and Tasks.
  https://docs.python.org/3/library/asyncio-task.html
- `time` - Time access and conversions.
  https://docs.python.org/3/library/time.html
- `random` - Generate pseudo-random numbers.
  https://docs.python.org/3/library/random.html

Next

In the next lesson, we will explore how to define, create and use asynchronous iterators, generators, and context managers.

Lesson 04: Iterators, Generators, and Context Managers

In this lesson, we will explore how to create and to use asynchronous iterators, generators, and context managers in asyncio programs. These are the asynchronous versions of the classical iterators, generators, and context managers we may use in conventional programs.

After completing this lesson, you will know:

- How to define, create and traverse asynchronous iterators and how they compare to classical iterators.
- How to create and use asynchronous generators and how they compare to classical generators.
- How to define and create asynchronous context managers and how they compare to classical context managers
- How and when to use the `async for` expression in coroutines with asynchronous iterables.
- How and when to use the `async with` expression for use with asynchronous context managers.

Let's get started.

How to Use Asynchronous Iterators

An asynchronous iterator is an object that implements the __aiter__() and __anext__() methods.

Before we take a close look at asynchronous iterators, let's review classical iterators and see how they compare to asynchronous iterators.

What are Classical and Asynchronous Iterators

An iterator is an object that implements a specific interface.

Specifically, the __iter__() method returns an instance of the iterator, and the __next__() method steps the iterator one cycle and returns a value.

An iterator can be stepped using the next() built-in function or traversed using a for-loop.

Many objects are iterable, most notable are containers such as lists.

An asynchronous iterator is an object that implements a specific interface, specifically the __aiter__() and __anext__() methods.

The __aiter__() method must return an instance of the iterator. The __anext__() method must return an awaitable that steps the iterator.

An asynchronous iterator may only be stepped or traversed in an asyncio program, such as within a coroutine.

An asynchronous iterator can be stepped using the anext() built-in function that returns an awaitable that executes one step of the iterator, e.g. one call to the __anext__() method.

An asynchronous iterator can be traversed using the async for expression that will automatically call anext() each iteration and await the returned awaitable in order to retrieve the return value. We will learn more about the async for expression in a moment.

Next, let's look at how to define an asynchronous iterator.

How to Define an Asynchronous Iterator

We can define an asynchronous iterator by defining a class that implements the `__aiter__()` and `__anext__()` methods.

These methods are defined on an object as per normal.

Importantly, because the `__anext__()` function must return an awaitable, it must be defined using the `async def` expression.

When the iteration is complete, the `__anext__()` method must raise a `StopAsyncIteration` exception.

For example:

```python
# define an asynchronous iterator
class AsyncIterator():
    # constructor, define some state
    def __init__(self):
        self.counter = 0

    # create an instance of the iterator
    def __aiter__(self):
        return self

    # return the next awaitable
    async def __anext__(self):
        # check for no further items
        if self.counter >= 10:
            raise StopAsyncIteration
        # increment the counter
        self.counter += 1
        # return the counter value
        return self.counter
```

Because the asynchronous iterator is a coroutine and each iterator returns an awaitable that is scheduled and executed in the asyncio event loop, we can execute and await awaitables within the body of the iterator.

For example:

```
...
# return the next awaitable
async def __anext__(self):
    # check for no further items
    if self.counter >= 10:
        raise StopAsyncIteration
    # increment the counter
    self.counter += 1
    # simulate work
    await asyncio.sleep(1)
    # return the counter value
    return self.counter
```

Next, let's look at how we can use an asynchronous iterator.

How to Create an Asynchronous Iterator

To use an asynchronous iterator we must create the iterator.

This involves creating the object as per normal.

For example:

```
...
# create the iterator
it = AsyncIterator()
```

This returns an *asynchronous iterable*, which is an instance of an *asynchronous iterator*.

Next, let's look at how to step an asynchronous iterator.

How to Step an Asynchronous Iterator

One step of the iterator can be traversed using the anext() built-in function, just like a classical iterator can be traversed using the next() function.

The result is an awaitable that is awaited.

For example:

```
...
# get an awaitable for one step of the iterator
awaitable = anext(it)
# execute the one step and get the result
result = await awaitable
```

This can be achieved on one line.

For example:

```
...
# step the async iterator
result = await anext(it)
```

Next, let's look at how to traverse an asynchronous iterator to completion.

How to Traverse an Asynchronous Iterator

The asynchronous iterator can also be traversed in a loop using the `async for` expression that will await each iteration of the loop automatically.

For example:

```
...
# traverse an asynchronous iterator
async for result in AsyncIterator():
    print(result)
```

This does not execute the for-loop in parallel. Instead, this is an asynchronous for-loop.

The difference is that the coroutine that executes the for-loop will suspend and internally `await` each awaitable iteration.

Behind the scenes, this may require coroutines to be scheduled and awaited, or tasks to be awaited.

An asynchronous iterator cannot be traversed using the `for` expression and classical iterators cannot be traversed using the `async for` expression. Each expression expects different methods to exist on the object that is being iterated.

We may also use an asynchronous list comprehension with the `async for` expression to collect the results of the iterator.

For example:

```
...
# async list comprehension with async iterator
results = [item async for item in AsyncIterator()]
```

This is called an asynchronous `list` comprehension. We may also use the `async for` expression in asynchronous `dict` and `set` comprehensions.

Now that we are familiar with how to create and use asynchronous iterators, let's look at a worked example.

Example of Using an Asynchronous Iterator

We can explore how to traverse an asynchronous iterator using the `async for` expression.

In this example, we will create and traverse the asynchronous iterator to completion using an `async for` loop.

This loop will automatically await each awaitable returned from the iterator, retrieve the returned value, and make it available within the loop body so that in this case it can be reported.

This is perhaps the most common usage pattern for asynchronous iterators.

The complete example is listed below.

```
# SuperFastPython.com
# example of an async iterator with async for loop
import asyncio

# define an asynchronous iterator
class AsyncIterator():
```

```python
    # constructor, define some state
    def __init__(self):
        self.counter = 0

    # create an instance of the iterator
    def __aiter__(self):
        return self

    # return the next awaitable
    async def __anext__(self):
        # check for no further items
        if self.counter >= 10:
            raise StopAsyncIteration
        # increment the counter
        self.counter += 1
        # simulate work
        await asyncio.sleep(1)
        # return the counter value
        return self.counter

# main coroutine
async def main():
    # loop over async iterator with async for loop
    async for item in AsyncIterator():
        print(item)

# execute the asyncio program
asyncio.run(main())
```

Running the example first creates the **main()** coroutine and uses it as the entry point into the asyncio program.

The **main()** coroutine runs and starts the for-loop.

An instance of the asynchronous iterator is created and the loop automatically steps it using the **anext()** function to return an await-able. The loop then awaits the awaitable and retrieves a value which is made available to the body of the loop where it is reported.

This process is then repeated, suspending the `main()` coroutine, executing a step of the iterator and suspending, and resuming the `main()` coroutine until the iterator is exhausted.

Once the internal counter of the iterator reaches 10, a `StopAsyncIteration` exception is raised. This does not terminate the program. Instead, it is expected and handled by the `async for` expression and breaks the loop.

This highlights how an asynchronous iterator can be traversed using an `async for` expression.

```
1
2
3
4
5
6
7
8
9
10
```

Next, let's look at how we can use asynchronous generators in asyncio programs.

How to Use Asynchronous Generators

An asynchronous generator is a coroutine that uses the `yield` expression.

Before we dive into the details of asynchronous generators, let's first review classical generators and see how they compare to asynchronous generators.

What are Classical and Asynchronous Generators

A generator is a function that returns a value via a `yield` expression.

For example:

```
# define a generator
def generator():
    for i in range(10):
        yield i
```

The generator is executed to the `yield` expression, after which a value is returned. This suspends the generator at that point. The next time the generator is executed it is resumed from the point it was suspended and runs until the next `yield` expression.

Technically, a generator function creates and returns a generator iterator. The generator iterator executes the content of the generator function, yielding and resuming as needed.

A generator can be executed in steps by using the `next()` built-in function.

For example:

```
...
# create the generator
gen = generator()
# step the generator
result = next(gen)
```

Although, it is more common to iterate the generator to completion, such as using a for-loop or a list comprehension.

For example:

```
...
# traverse the generator and collect results
results = [item for item in generator()]
```

An asynchronous generator is a coroutine that uses the `yield` expression.

Unlike a function generator, the coroutine can schedule and await other coroutines and tasks.

Like a classical generator, an asynchronous generator function can be used to create an asynchronous generator iterator that can be traversed using the built-in `anext()` function, instead of the `next()` function.

This means that the asynchronous generator iterator implements the `__anext__()` method and can be used with the `async for` expression.

Each iteration of the generator is scheduled and executed as awaitable. The `async for` expression will schedule and execute each iteration of the generator, suspending the calling coroutine and awaiting the result.

Next, let's explore how we can define an asynchronous generator.

How to Define an Asynchronous Generator

We can define an asynchronous generator by defining a coroutine that has at least one `yield` expression.

This means that the function is defined using the `async def` expression.

For example:

```
# define an asynchronous generator
async def async_generator():
    for i in range(10)
        yield i
```

Because the asynchronous generator is a coroutine and each iterator returns an awaitable that is scheduled and executed in the asyncio event loop, we can execute and await awaitables within the body of the generator.

For example:

```
# define an asynchronous generator that awaits
async def async_generator():
    for i in range(10)
        # suspend and sleep a moment
```

```
    await asyncio.sleep(1)
    # yield a value to the caller
    yield i
```

Next, let's look at how we create an asynchronous generator.

How to Create Asynchronous Generator

To use an asynchronous generator we must create the generator.

This looks like calling the generator but instead creates and returns an iterator object, called an iterable.

For example:

```
...
# create the iterator
it = async_generator()
```

This returns a type of asynchronous iterator called an asynchronous generator iterator.

Next, let's look at how we can step an asynchronous generator.

How to Step an Asynchronous Generator

One step of the generator can be traversed using the **anext()** built-in function, just like a classical generator using the **next()** function.

The result is an awaitable that can be awaited.

For example:

```
...
# get an awaitable for one step of the generator
awaitable = anext(gen)
# execute the one step of the gen and get the result
result = await awaitable
```

This can be achieved in one step.

For example:

```
...
# step the async generator
result = await anext(gen)
```

Next, let's look at how we can traverse an asynchronous generator.

How to Traverse an Asynchronous Generator

The asynchronous generator can also be traversed in a loop using the `async for` expression that will await each iteration of the loop automatically.

For example:

```
...
# traverse an asynchronous generator
async for result in async_generator():
    print(result)
```

We may also use an asynchronous list comprehension with the `async for` expression to collect the results of the generator.

For example:

```
...
# async list comprehension with async generator
results = [item async for item in async_generator()]
```

Now that we know how to create and use asynchronous generators, let's look at a worked example.

Example of Using an Asynchronous Generator

We can explore how to traverse an asynchronous generator using the `async for` expression.

In this example, we will create and traverse the asynchronous generator to completion using an `async for` loop.

This loop will automatically await each awaitable returned from the generator, retrieve the yielded value, and make it available within the loop body so that in this case it can be reported.

This is perhaps the most common usage pattern for asynchronous generators.

The complete example is listed below.

```
# SuperFastPython.com
# example of asynchronous generator with async for loop
import asyncio

# define an asynchronous generator
async def async_generator():
    # normal loop
    for i in range(10):
        # suspend to simulate doing work
        await asyncio.sleep(1)
        # yield the result
        yield i

# main coroutine
async def main():
    # loop over async generator with async for loop
    async for item in async_generator():
        print(item)

# execute the asyncio program
asyncio.run(main())
```

Running the example first creates the `main()` coroutine and uses it as the entry point into the asyncio program.

The `main()` coroutine runs and starts the for-loop.

An instance of the asynchronous generator is created and the loop automatically steps it using the `anext()` function to return an await-able. The loop then awaits the awaitable and retrieves a value which is made available to the body of the loop where it is reported.

This process is then repeated, suspending the `main()` coroutine, executing an iteration of the generator, and suspending, and resuming the `main()` coroutine until the generator is exhausted.

This highlights how an asynchronous generator can be traversed using an `async for` expression.

```
0
1
2
3
4
5
6
7
8
9
```

Next, let's look at how to use asynchronous context managers in our asyncio programs.

How to Use Asynchronous Context Managers

An asynchronous context manager is an object that implements the `__aenter__()` and `__aexit__()` methods.

Before we dive into the details of asynchronous context managers, let's review classical context managers and see how they compare to asynchronous context managers.

What are Classical and Asynchronous Context Managers

A context manager is an object that implements the `__enter__()` and `__exit__()` methods.

The `__enter__()` method defines what happens at the beginning of a code block, such as opening or preparing resources, like a file, socket, or thread pool.

The `__exit__()` method defines what happens when the code block is exited, such as closing a prepared resource.

Typically a context manager object is created at the beginning of the `with` expression and the `__enter__()` method is called automatically. The body of the content makes use of the resource via the named context manager object, then the `__aexit__()` method is called automatically when the code block is exited, normally, or via an exception.

For example:

```
...
# open a context manager
with ContextManager() as manager:
    # ...
# closed automatically
```

This mirrors a try-finally expression.

For example:

```
...
# create the object
manager = ContextManager()
try:
    manager.__enter__()
    # ...
finally:
    manager.__exit__()
```

Asynchronous context managers provide a context manager that can be suspended when entering and exiting.

The `__aenter__()` and `__aexit__()` methods are defined as coroutines and are awaited by the caller.

This is achieved using the `async with` expression which we will learn more about in a moment.

As such, asynchronous context managers can only be used within asyncio programs, such as within calling coroutines.

Next, let's take a closer look at how to define an asynchronous context manager.

How to Define an Asynchronous Context Manager

We can define an asynchronous context manager as an object that implements the __aenter__() and __aexit__() methods.

Importantly, both methods must be defined as coroutines using the async def expression and therefore must return awaitables.

For example:

```
# define an asynchronous context manager
class AsyncContextManager:
    # enter the async context manager
    async def __aenter__(self):
        # report a message
        print('>entering the context manager')

    # exit the async context manager
    async def __aexit__(self, exc_type, exc, tb):
        # report a message
        print('>exiting the context manager')
```

Because each of the methods are coroutines, they may themselves await coroutines or tasks.

For example:

```
# define an asynchronous context manager
class AsyncContextManager:
    # enter the async context manager
    async def __aenter__(self):
        # report a message
        print('>entering the context manager')
        # suspend for a moment
        await asyncio.sleep(0.5)

    # exit the async context manager
    async def __aexit__(self, exc_type, exc, tb):
```

```
# report a message
print('>exiting the context manager')
# suspend for a moment
await asyncio.sleep(0.5)
```

Next, let's look at how we can create and use an asynchronous context manager.

How to Use an Asynchronous Context Manager

A asynchronous context manager is used via the `async with` expression.

This is an extension of the `with` expression for use in coroutines.

It will automatically await the enter and exit coroutines, suspending the calling coroutine as needed.

For example:

```
...
# use an asynchronous context manager
async with AsyncContextManager() as manager:
    # ...
```

This is equivalent to something like:

```
...
# create or enter the async context manager
manager = await AsyncContextManager()
try:
    # ...
finally:
    # close or exit the context manager
    await manager.close()
```

An asynchronous context manager cannot be used via the `with` expression and a classical context manager cannot be used via the `async with` expression. Each expression expects different methods to exist on the target object.

Notice that we are implementing much the same pattern as a traditional context manager, except that creating and closing the context manager involve awaiting coroutines.

This suspends the execution of the current coroutine, schedules a new coroutine, and waits for it to complete.

As such an asynchronous context manager must implement the `__aenter__()` and `__aexit__()` methods that must be defined via the `async def` expression. This makes them coroutines themselves which may also await.

Now that we know how to use asynchronous context managers, let's look at a worked example.

Example of Using an Asynchronous Context Manager

We can explore how to use an asynchronous context manager via the `async with` expression.

In this example, we will create and use the context manager in a normal manner.

We will use an `async with` expression and on one line, create and enter the context manager. This will automatically await the enter method.

We can then make use of the manager within the inner code block. In this case, we will just report a message.

Exiting the inner code block will automatically await the exit method of the context manager.

The complete example is listed below.

```
# SuperFastPython.com
# example of an async context manager via async with
import asyncio

# define an asynchronous context manager
```

```python
class AsyncContextManager:
    # enter the async context manager
    async def __aenter__(self):
        # report a message
        print('>entering the context manager')
        # suspend for a moment
        await asyncio.sleep(0.5)

    # exit the async context manager
    async def __aexit__(self, exc_type, exc, tb):
        # report a message
        print('>exiting the context manager')
        # suspend for a moment
        await asyncio.sleep(0.5)

# define a simple coroutine
async def custom_coroutine():
    # create and use the asynchronous context manager
    async with AsyncContextManager() as manager:
        # report the result
        print('within the manager')

# start the asyncio program
asyncio.run(custom_coroutine())
```

Running the example first creates the `main()` coroutine and uses it as the entry point into the asyncio program.

The `main()` coroutine runs and creates an instance of our `AsyncContextManager` class in an `async with` expression.

This expression automatically calls the enter method and awaits the coroutine. A message is reported and the coroutine suspends for a moment.

The `main()` coroutine resumes and executes the body of the context manager, printing a message.

The code block is exited and the exit method of the context manager is awaited automatically, reporting a message and sleeping a moment.

This highlights the normal usage pattern for an asynchronous context manager in an asyncio program.

```
>entering the context manager
within the manager
>exiting the context manager
```

Lesson Review

Takeaways

Well done, you made it to the end of the lesson.

- You now know how to define, create and traverse asynchronous iterators and how they compare to classical iterators.
- You now know how to create and use asynchronous generators and how they compare to classical generators.
- You now know how to define and create asynchronous context managers and how they compare to classical context managers
- You now know how and when to use the `async for` expression in coroutines with asynchronous iterables.
- You now know how and when to use the `async with` expression for use with asynchronous context managers.

Exercise

Your task in this lesson is to use what you have learned about asynchronous iterators.

Develop an asynchronous iterator that traverses some arbitrary data structure. You can develop an asynchronous generator if you prefer.

Ensure that the coroutine executed each step does some work or simulated work such as a sleep.

Create and traverse the iterator in the main loop of your asyncio program using the `async for` expression.

Update your example to use an asynchronous list comprehension to traverse the iterator.

This will help make you more comfortable with asynchronous loops and iteration. There is a lot of general confusion about the `async for` expression and you will better understand what it is doing by developing your own asynchronous iterators and generators.

Share your results online on Twitter, LinkedIn, GitHub, or similar.

Send me the link to your results, I'd love to see what you come up with.

You can send me a message directly via:

- Super Fast Python - Contact Page
  https://SuperFastPython.com/contact/

Or share it with me on Twitter via @SuperFastPython.

Further Reading

This section provides resources for you to learn more about the topics covered in this lesson.

- `asyncio` - Asynchronous I/O.
  https://docs.python.org/3/library/asyncio.html
- PEP 525 - Asynchronous Generators.
  https://peps.python.org/pep-0525/
- PEP 530 - Asynchronous Comprehensions.
  https://peps.python.org/pep-0530/
- Python Compound statements.
  https://docs.python.org/3/reference/compound_stmts.html

Next

In the next lesson, we will explore how to synchronize and coordinate coroutines and how to share data between coroutines.

Lesson 05: Queues and Synchronization Primitives

In this lesson, we will explore how to share data between coroutines using queues and how to use concurrency primitives to synchronize and coordinate coroutines in our asyncio programs.

After completing this lesson, you will know:

- How to use coroutine-safe queues to share data between coroutines.
- How to use mutex locks to protect critical sections from race conditions.
- How to use semaphores to limit concurrent access to a resource for coroutines.
- How to use an event to signal between coroutines.
- How to coordinate coroutines with wait and notify using a condition variable.

Let's get started.

What is Coroutine-Safe

Thread-safe refers to program code that can be executed free of concurrency errors by multiple threads concurrently.

Primarily, it refers to the fact that the code is free of race conditions.

A race condition is a bug in concurrency programming. It is a failure case where the behavior of the program is dependent upon the order of execution by two or more threads. This means the behavior of the program will be unpredictable, possibly changing each time it is run.

Process-safe refers to program code that can be executed free of concurrency errors by multiple processes concurrently. It is the concept of *thread-safe* applied to processes, where processes are the unit of concurrency instead of threads.

As such, coroutine-safe is the idea of *thread-safe* and *process-safe* applied to coroutines.

Although two or more coroutines cannot execute at the same time within the event loop, it is possible for program state and resources to be corrupted or made inconsistent via concurrent execution.

Coroutine-safe means that code or a program can be executed concurrently with multiple coroutines and will not result in concurrency failure modes such as race conditions.

The `asyncio` module provides a number of concurrency primitives that are coroutine-safe.

This lesson will focus of ways to share data, protect data, and coordinate behavior between coroutines that is coroutine-safe.

How to Share Data Between Coroutines with Queues

A queue can be used to share data between coroutines.

A queue is a coroutine-safe data structure that can be used to share data between coroutines without a race condition.

The `asyncio` module provides the `asyncio.Queue` class for general use, but also provides a last-in-first-out (LIFO) queue via the `asyncio.LifoQueue` class and a priority queue via the `asyncio.PriorityQueue` class.

A queue is a data structure on which items can be added by a call to put() and from which items can be retrieved by a call to get().

Coroutine-safe means that it can be used by multiple coroutines to put and get items concurrently without a race condition.

The Queue class provides a first-in, first-out FIFO queue, which means that the items are retrieved from the queue in the order they were added. The first items added to the queue will be the first items retrieved.

Next, let's look at how to use queues in asyncio programs.

How to Use Asyncio Queues

The asyncio.Queue can be used by first creating an instance of the class. This will create an unbounded queue by default, that is, a queue with no size limit.

For example:

```
...
# created an unbounded queue
queue = asyncio.Queue()
```

A maximum capacity can be set on a new Queue via the maxsize constructor augment.

For example:

```
...
# created a queue with a maximum capacity
queue = asyncio.Queue(maxsize=100)
```

Items can be added to the queue via a call to the put() method. This is a coroutine that must be awaited, suspending the caller until the item can be placed on the queue successfully. For example:

```
...
# add an item to the queue
await queue.put(item)
```

If a size-limited queue becomes full, new items cannot be added and calls to put() will suspend until space becomes available.

Items can be retrieved from the queue by calls to get(). This is also a coroutine and must be awaited, suspending the caller until an item can be retrieved from the queue successfully.

For example:

```
...
# get an item from the queue
item = await queue.get()
```

Now that we know how to use queues, let's look at a worked example of sharing data between coroutines.

Example of Producer and Consumer Tasks with a Queue

We can explore an example of sharing data between two coroutines using a queue.

In this example, we will define a custom task function that takes the queue as an argument, generates some data, and puts that data on the queue. It is a producer coroutine.

The main coroutine will create the queue, share it with the new coroutine and then suspend, waiting for data to arrive on the queue. The main coroutine will be the consumer coroutine.

The complete example of sharing data between coroutines using a queue is listed below.

```
# SuperFastPython.com
# example of producer/consumer connected via a queue
from random import random
import asyncio

# coroutine to generate work
async def producer(queue):
    print('Producer: Running')
```

```python
    # generate work
    for _ in range(10):
        # generate a value
        value = random()
        # suspend to simulate work
        await asyncio.sleep(value)
        # add to the queue
        await queue.put(value)
    # send an all done signal
    await queue.put(None)
    print('Producer: Done')

# coroutine to consume work
async def consumer(queue):
    print('Consumer: Running')
    # consume work
    while True:
        # get a unit of work
        item = await queue.get()
        # check for stop signal
        if item is None:
            break
        # report
        print(f'>got {item}')
    # all done
    print('Consumer: Done')

# entry point coroutine
async def main():
    # create the shared queue
    queue = asyncio.Queue()
    # run the producer and consumers
    await asyncio.gather(
        producer(queue), consumer(queue))

# start the asyncio program
```

```
asyncio.run(main())
```

Running the example first creates the `main()` coroutine and uses it as the entry point into the asyncio program.

The `main()` coroutine runs and the shared `asyncio.Queue` object is then created.

Next, the producer coroutine is created and passed the queue instance. Then the consumer coroutine is started and the main coroutine suspends until both coroutines terminate.

The producer coroutine generates a new random value for each iteration of the task, suspends, and adds it to the queue. The consumer coroutine waits on the queue for items to arrive, then consumes them one at a time, reporting their value.

Finally, the producer task finishes, a `None` value is put on the queue and the coroutine terminates. The consumer coroutine gets the `None` value, breaks its loop, and also terminates.

This highlights how the `asyncio.Queue` can be used to share data easily between producer and consumer coroutines.

NOTE: Results will vary each time the program is run given the use of random numbers.

```
Producer: Running
Consumer: Running
>got 0.7559246569022605
>got 0.965203750033905
>got 0.49834912260024233
>got 0.22783211775499135
>got 0.07775542407106295
>got 0.5997647474647314
>got 0.7236540952500915
>got 0.7956407178426339
>got 0.11256095725867177
Producer: Done
>got 0.9095338767572713
```

Consumer: Done

Next, let's look at how we can use mutex locks in our asyncio programs.

How to Protect Critical Sections with a Mutex Lock

A mutual exclusion lock, or mutex lock for short, is a concurrency primitive intended to prevent a race condition.

A race condition is a concurrency failure case when two coroutines run the same code and access or update the same resource (e.g. data variables, stream, etc.) leaving the resource in an unknown and inconsistent state.

Race conditions often result in unexpected behavior of a program and/or corrupt data.

These sensitive parts of code that can be executed by multiple coroutines concurrently and may result in race conditions are called critical sections. A critical section may refer to a single block of code, but it also refers to multiple accesses to the same data variable or resource from multiple functions.

Next, let's look at how we can use mutex locks.

How to Use an Asyncio Lock

Python provides a mutual exclusion lock for use with coroutines via the `asyncio.Lock` class.

An instance of the `Lock` class can be created and then acquired by coroutines before accessing a critical section, and released after exiting the critical section.

The `acquire()` method is used to acquire the lock. It is a coroutine and must be awaited, suspending the calling coroutine. The lock can be released again later via the `release()` method.

For example:

```
...
# create a lock
lock = asyncio.Lock()
# acquire the lock
await lock.acquire()
# ...
# release the lock
lock.release()
```

Only one coroutine can have the lock at any time. If a coroutine does not release an acquired lock, it cannot be acquired again.

The coroutine attempting to acquire the lock will suspend until the lock is acquired, such as if another coroutine currently holds the lock then releases it.

We can also use the lock via the context manager interface via the `async with` expression, allowing the critical section to be a block of code within the context manager and for the lock to be released automatically once the block of code is exited, normally or otherwise.

For example:

```
...
# create a lock
lock = asyncio.Lock()
# acquire the lock
async with lock:
    # ...
```

This is the preferred usage of the lock as it makes it clear where the protected code begins and ends, and ensures that the lock is always released, even if there is an exception or error within the critical section.

Now that we know how to use mutex locks, let's look at a worked example.

Example of Using an Asyncio Lock

We can develop an example to demonstrate how to use the mutex lock.

In this example, we will define a target task that takes a lock as an argument and uses the lock to protect a critical section, which in this case will print a message and sleep for a moment.

The complete example is listed below.

```python
# SuperFastPython.com
# example of an asyncio mutual exclusion (mutex) lock
from random import random
import asyncio

# task coroutine with a critical section
async def task(lock, num, value):
    # acquire the lock to protect the critical section
    async with lock:
        # report a message
        print(f'>{num} got the lock, sleep for {value}')
        # suspend for a moment
        await asyncio.sleep(value)

# entry point
async def main():
    # create a shared lock
    lock = asyncio.Lock()
    # create many concurrent coroutines
    coros = [task(lock, i, random()) for i in range(10)]
    # execute and wait for tasks to complete
    await asyncio.gather(*coros)

# run the asyncio program
asyncio.run(main())
```

Running the example first creates the `main()` coroutine and uses it as the entry point into the asyncio program.

The `main()` coroutine runs, first creating the shared lock.

It then creates a list of coroutines, each is passed the shared lock, a unique integer, and a random floating point value.

The list of coroutines is passed to the `gather()` function and the `main()` coroutine suspends until all coroutines are completed.

A task coroutine executes, acquires the lock, reports a message, then awaits the sleep, suspending.

Another coroutine resumes. It attempts to acquire the lock and is suspended, while it waits. This process is repeated with many if not all coroutines.

The first coroutines resumes, exits the block of code, and releases the lock automatically via the asynchronous context manager.

The first coroutine to wait on the lock resumes, acquires the lock, reports a message, and sleeps.

This process repeats until all coroutines are given an opportunity to acquire the lock, execute the critical section and terminate.

Once all tasks terminate, the `main()` coroutine resumes and terminates, closing the program.

NOTE: Results will vary each time the program is run given the use of random numbers.

```
>coroutine 0 got the lock, sleeping for 0.35342849008361
>coroutine 1 got the lock, sleeping for 0.78996044707365
>coroutine 2 got the lock, sleeping for 0.10018104240779
>coroutine 3 got the lock, sleeping for 0.75009875150084
>coroutine 4 got the lock, sleeping for 0.54066805101353
>coroutine 5 got the lock, sleeping for 0.53074317625936
>coroutine 6 got the lock, sleeping for 0.44269144160147
>coroutine 7 got the lock, sleeping for 0.79732810383210
>coroutine 8 got the lock, sleeping for 0.49827720719979
>coroutine 9 got the lock, sleeping for 0.18177356607777
```

Next, let's look at how we can use semaphores in our asyncio programs.

How to Limit Access to a Resource with a Semaphore

A semaphore is a concurrency primitive that allows a limit on the number of coroutines that can acquire a lock protecting a critical section or resource.

It is an extension of a mutual exclusion (mutex) lock that adds a count for the number of coroutines that can acquire the lock before additional coroutines will suspend. Once full, new coroutines can only acquire access on the semaphore once an existing coroutine holding the semaphore releases access.

Internally, the semaphore maintains a counter protected by a mutex lock that is decremented each time the semaphore is acquired and incremented each time it is released. When a semaphore is created, the upper limit on the counter is set. If it is set to 1, then the semaphore will operate like a mutex lock.

Next, let's look at how we can create and use a semaphore.

How to Use an Asyncio Semaphore

Python provides a semaphore for coroutines via the `asyncio.Semaphore` class.

The `Semaphore` object must be configured when it is created to set the limit on the internal counter. This limit will match the number of concurrent coroutines that can hold the semaphore.

For example, we can set it to 100:

```
...
# create a semaphore with a limit of 100
semaphore = asyncio.Semaphore(100)
```

Each time the `Semaphore` is acquired, the internal counter is decremented. Each time the `Semaphore` is released, the internal counter is incremented.

The `Semaphore` cannot be acquired if it has no available positions (e.g. the count is zero) in which case, threads attempting to acquire it must suspend until a position becomes available.

The semaphore can be acquired by calling the `acquire()` method which must be awaited.

For example:

```
...
# acquire the semaphore
await semaphore.acquire()
```

By default, the calling coroutine will suspend until access becomes available on the semaphore.

Once acquired, the semaphore can be released again by calling the `release()` method.

For example:

```
...
# release the semaphore
semaphore.release()
```

The `Semaphore` class supports usage via the context manager, which will automatically acquire and release the semaphore for us. As such it is the preferred way to use semaphores in our programs.

For example:

```
...
# acquire the semaphore
async with semaphore:
    # ...
```

Now that we know how to use semaphores, let's look at a worked example.

Example of Using an Asyncio Semaphore

We can explore how to use a `asyncio.Semaphore` with a worked example.

In this example, we will start a suite of coroutines but limit the number that can perform an action simultaneously. A semaphore will be used to limit the number of concurrent tasks that may execute which will be less than the total number of coroutines, allowing some coroutines to suspend, wait for access, then be notified and acquire access.

The complete example is listed below.

```python
# SuperFastPython.com
# example of using an asyncio semaphore
from random import random
import asyncio

# task coroutine
async def task(semaphore, number):
    # acquire the semaphore
    async with semaphore:
        # generate a random value between 0 and 1
        value = random()
        # suspend for a moment
        await asyncio.sleep(value)
        # report a message
        print(f'Task {number} got {value}')

# main coroutine
async def main():
    # create the shared semaphore
    semaphore = asyncio.Semaphore(2)
    # create and schedule tasks
    tasks = [asyncio.create_task(task(semaphore, i))
        for i in range(10)]
    # wait for all tasks to complete
    _ = await asyncio.wait(tasks)
```

```
# start the asyncio program
asyncio.run(main())
```

Running the example first creates the `main()` coroutine that is used as the entry point into the asyncio program.

The `main()` coroutine runs and first creates the shared semaphore with an initial counter value of 2, meaning that two coroutines can hold the semaphore at once.

The `main()` coroutine then creates and schedules 10 tasks to execute our `task()` coroutine, passing the shared semaphore and a unique number between 0 and 9.

The `main()` coroutine then suspends and waits for all tasks to complete.

The tasks run one at a time.

Each task first attempts to acquire the semaphore. If there is a position available it proceeds, otherwise it waits for a position to become available.

Once acquired, a task generates a random value, suspend for a moment, and then reports the generated value. It then releases the semaphore and terminates. The semaphore is not released while the task is suspended in the call to `asyncio.sleep()`.

The body of the semaphore context manager is limited to two semaphores at a time.

This highlights how we can limit the number of coroutines to execute a block of code concurrently.

NOTE: Results will vary each time the program is run given the use of random numbers.

```
Task 0 got 0.20369168197618748
Task 2 got 0.20640107131350838
Task 1 got 0.6855263719449817
Task 3 got 0.9396433586858612
```

```
Task 4 got 0.8039832235015294
Task 6 got 0.12266060196253203
Task 5 got 0.879466225105295
Task 7 got 0.6675244153844875
Task 8 got 0.11511060306129695
Task 9 got 0.9607702805925814
```

Next, let's look at how to use events in asyncio programs.

How to Signal Between Coroutines Using an Event

An event is a coroutine-safe boolean flag that can be used to signal between two or more coroutines.

It can be useful to coordinate the behavior of many coroutines that can check the status of the flag, such as to begin processing, or to stop processing and exit.

Next, let's look at how to create and use events.

How to Use an Asyncio Event

Python provides an event object for coroutines via the `asyncio.Event` class.

An `Event` class wraps a boolean variable that can either be *set* (`True`) or *not set* (`False`). Coroutines sharing the `Event` object can check if the event is set, set the event, clear the event (make it not set), or wait for the event to be set.

The `Event` provides an easy way to share a boolean variable between coroutines that can act as a trigger for an action.

First, an `Event` object must be created and the event will be in the *not set* state.

```
...
# create an instance of an event
event = asyncio.Event()
```

Once created we can check if the event has been set via the `is_set()` method which will return `True` if the event is set, or `False` otherwise.

For example:

```
...
# check if the event is set
if event.is_set():
    # do something...
```

The `Event` can be set via the `set()` method. Any coroutines waiting on the event to be set will be notified.

For example:

```
...
# set the event
event.set()
```

Finally, coroutines can wait for the event to be set via the `wait()` method, which must be awaited. Calling this method will suspend until the event is marked as set (e.g. another coroutine calling the `set()` method). If the event is already set, the `wait()` method will return immediately.

```
...
# wait for the event to be set
await event.wait()
```

Now that we know to use events, let's look at a worked example.

Example of Using an Asyncio Event

We can explore how to use an `asyncio.Event` object.

In this example we will create a suite of coroutines that each will perform some work and report a message. All coroutines will use an event to wait to be set before starting their work. The main coroutine will set the event and trigger the new coroutines to start work.

```python
# SuperFastPython.com
# example of using an asyncio event object
from random import random
import asyncio

# task coroutine
async def task(event, number):
    # wait for the event to be set
    await event.wait()
    # generate a random value between 0 and 1
    value = random()
    # suspend for a moment
    await asyncio.sleep(value)
    # report a message
    print(f'Task {number} got {value}')

# main coroutine
async def main():
    # create a shared event object
    event = asyncio.Event()
    # create and run the tasks
    tasks = [asyncio.create_task(task(event, i))
        for i in range(5)]
    # allow the tasks to start
    print('Main suspending...')
    await asyncio.sleep(0)
    # start processing in all tasks
    print('Main setting the event')
    event.set()
    # await for all tasks  to terminate
    _ = await asyncio.wait(tasks)

# run the asyncio program
asyncio.run(main())
```

Running the example first creates the `main()` coroutine and uses it as the entry point into the asyncio program.

The `main()` coroutine runs and creates and schedules five task coroutines.

It then sleeps, suspending and allowing the tasks to run and start waiting on the event.

The main coroutine resumes, reports a message then sets the event to `True`. It then suspends and waits for all issued tasks to complete.

This triggers all five coroutines. They resume in turn perform their processing and report a message.

This highlights how coroutines can wait for an event to be set and how we can notify coroutines using an event.

NOTE: Results will vary each time the program is run given the use of random numbers.

```
Main suspending...
Main setting the event
Task 3 got 0.36705703414223256
Task 1 got 0.4852630342496812
Task 0 got 0.7251916806567016
Task 4 got 0.8104350284043036
Task 2 got 0.9726611709531982
```

Next, let's look at how we can use condition variables in asyncio programs.

How to Coordinate Using a Condition Variable

A condition variable, also called a monitor, allows multiple coroutines to wait and be notified about some result.

A condition can be acquired by a coroutine after which it can wait to be notified by another coroutine that something has changed.

While waiting, the coroutine is suspended and releases the lock on the condition for other coroutines to acquire.

Another coroutine can then acquire the condition, make a change in the program, and notify one, all, or a subset of coroutines waiting on the condition that something has changed.

The waiting coroutine can then resume, re-acquire the condition, perform checks on any changed state and perform required actions.

Next, let's look at how we can create and use condition variables.

How to Use an Asyncio Condition

Python provides a condition variable via the `asyncio.Condition` class.

For example:

```
...
# create a new condition variable
condition = asyncio.Condition()
```

In order for a coroutine to make use of the `Condition`, it must acquire it and release it, like a mutex lock.

This can be achieved manually with the `acquire()` and `release()` methods. The `acquire()` method is a coroutine and must be awaited.

For example, we can acquire the `Condition` and then wait on the condition to be notified and finally release the condition as follows:

```
...
# acquire the condition
await condition.acquire()
# wait to be notified
await condition.wait()
# release the condition
condition.release()
```

The `wait()` method is also a coroutine and must be awaited.

An alternative to calling the `acquire()` and `release()` methods directly is to use the context manager, which will perform the acquire and release automatically for us, for example:

```
...
# acquire the condition
async with condition:
    # wait to be notified
    await condition.wait()
```

We also must acquire the condition in a coroutine if we wish to notify waiting coroutines. This too can be achieved directly with the acquire and release methods calls or via the context manager.

We can notify a single waiting coroutine via the `notify()` method.

For example:

```
...
# acquire the condition
with condition:
    # notify a waiting coroutines
    condition.notify()
```

The notified coroutine will stop waiting as soon as it can reacquire the condition. This will be attempted automatically as part of its call to `wait()`, we do not need to do anything extra.

We can notify all coroutines waiting on the condition via the `notify_all()` method.

```
...
# acquire the condition
with condition:
    # notify all coroutines waiting on the condition
    condition.notify_all()
```

Now that we know how to use condition variables, let's look at a worked example.

Example of Using an Asyncio Condition

In this example, we will explore using an `asyncio.Condition` to notify a waiting coroutine that something has happened.

We will use a task to prepare some data and notify a waiting coroutine. In the main coroutine, we will create and schedule the new task and use the condition to wait for the work to be completed.

The complete example is listed below.

```python
# SuperFastPython.com
# example of wait/notify with an asyncio condition
import asyncio

# task coroutine
async def task(condition, work_list):
    # suspend for a moment
    await asyncio.sleep(1)
    # add data to the work list
    work_list.append(33)
    # notify a waiting coroutine that the work is done
    print('Task sending notification...')
    async with condition:
        condition.notify()

# main coroutine
async def main():
    # create a condition
    condition = asyncio.Condition()
    # prepare the work list
    work_list = []
    # wait to be notified that the data is ready
    print('Main waiting for data...')
    async with condition:
        # create and start the task
        _ = asyncio.create_task(
            task(condition, work_list))
        # wait to be notified
```

```
    await condition.wait()
    # we know the data is ready
    print(f'Got data: {work_list}')

# run the asyncio program
asyncio.run(main())
```

Running the example first creates the `main()` coroutine which is used as the entry point into the asyncio program.

The `main()` coroutine runs and creates the shared condition and the work list.

The `main()` coroutine then acquires the condition. A new task is created and scheduled, provided the shared condition and work list.

The `main()` coroutine then waits to be notified, suspending and calling the new scheduled task to run.

The `task()` coroutine runs. It first suspends for a moment to simulate effort, then adds work to the shared list. The condition is acquired and the waiting coroutine is notified, then releases the condition automatically. The task terminates.

The `main()` coroutine resumes and reports a final message, showing the updated content of the shared list.

This highlights how we can use a wait-notify pattern between coroutines using a condition variable.

```
Main waiting for data...
Task sending notification...
Got data: [33]
```

Lesson Review

Takeaways

Well done, you made it to the end of the lesson.

- You now know how to use coroutine-safe queues to share data between coroutines.
- You now know how to use mutex locks to protect critical sections from race conditions.
- You now know how to use semaphores to limit concurrent access to a resource for coroutines.
- You now know how to use an event to signal between coroutines.
- You now know how to coordinate coroutines with wait and notify using a condition variable.

Exercise

Your task for this lesson is to use what you have learned about concurrency primitives.

Develop a program where multiple tasks add and subtract from a single shared integer value.

You could have one or more tasks that add one to a balance many times each in a loop, and one or more tasks do the same by subtracting one from the same shared global variable.

Have each task that modifies the global balance variable give many opportunities for other coroutines to run, forcing a race condition.

For example:

```python
# coroutine to add to the shared balance
async def add():
    global balance
    for i in range(10000):
        tmp = balance
        await asyncio.sleep(0)
        tmp = tmp + 1
        await asyncio.sleep(0)
        balance = tmp

# coroutine to subtract from the shared balance
async def subtract():
```

```
global balance
for i in range(10000):
    tmp = balance
    await asyncio.sleep(0)
    tmp = tmp - 1
    await asyncio.sleep(0)
    balance = tmp
```

Confirm that the program results in a race condition by running the example multiple times and getting different results.

Update the example to be coroutine-safe and no longer suffer the race condition. Try a mutex lock. Also try a semaphore.

It is important that you experience a race condition in asyncio programs. Many developers falsely believe that race conditions are not possible in Python or are not something they need to worry about in asyncio with coroutines. Once you see one for yourself and know how to fix it, you will be able to bring this confidence with you into your future projects.

Share your results online on Twitter, LinkedIn, GitHub, or similar.

Send me the link to your results, I'd love to see what you come up with.

You can send me a message directly via:

- Super Fast Python - Contact Page
  https://SuperFastPython.com/contact/

Or share it with me on Twitter via @SuperFastPython.

Further Reading

This section provides resources for you to learn more about the topics covered in this lesson.

- asyncio - Asynchronous I/O.
  https://docs.python.org/3/library/asyncio.html

- Asyncio Synchronization Primitives.
  https://docs.python.org/3/library/asyncio-sync.html
- Asyncio Queues.
  https://docs.python.org/3/library/asyncio-queue.html
- Race condition, Wikipedia.
  https://en.wikipedia.org/wiki/Race_condition
- Mutual exclusion, Wikipedia.
  https://en.wikipedia.org/wiki/Mutual_exclusion
- Semaphore (programming), Wikipedia.
  https://en.wikipedia.org/wiki/Semaphore_(programming)
- Monitor (synchronization), Wikipedia.
  https://en.wikipedia.org/wiki/Monitor_(synchronization)
- `random` - Generate pseudo-random numbers.
  https://docs.python.org/3/library/random.html

Next

In the next lesson, we will explore how to run commands in subprocesses and create, read from and write to streams asynchronously.

Lesson 06: Subprocesses and Streams

In this lesson, we will explore how to run commands from an asyncio program in subprocesses. We will also explore how we can implement socket programming, such as opening a TCP socket connection then read and write from it asynchronous using non-blocking I/O.

After completing this lesson, you will know:

- How to run commands asynchronously as subprocesses directly from coroutines.
- How to run commands asynchronously using the shell from coroutines.
- How to open, read, and write from non-blocking TCP socket connections.
- How to check the status of webpages asynchronously using streams.

Let's get started.

How to Run Commands in Subprocesses

The `asyncio` module provides an API for running commands on the underlying system asynchronously.

Commands can be called directly or executed via the user's shell and will execute in a subprocess.

Asyncio programs can then control the command running in a subprocess by asynchronously reading data from the subprocess, asynchronously writing data to subprocess, and killing the subprocess if need be.

Before we explore how to run commands as subprocesses, let's review a command, the shell, and why we want to execute commands a subprocesses.

What is a Command and a Shell

A command is a program executed on the command line (terminal or command prompt). It is another program that is run directly.

Common examples on Linux and macOS are:

- `ls` to list the contents of a directory.
- `cat` to report the content of a file.
- `date` to report the date.
- `echo` to report back a string.
- `sleep` to sleep for a number of seconds.

And so on.

These are just programs that we can execute on the command line as a command.

We may want to execute a command from our program for many reasons.

For example:

- We may want to change the permissions of a file or change a system configuration.
- We may want to run a program to check the status of a resource or value of a system property.
- We may want to start another program in the background or for the user to interact with.

Many actions performed by external commands may be executed directly by Python using the standard library API or a third-party library. Sometimes it can be easier to simply run a purpose-made command directly on the operating system.

We can execute these commands using the shell.

The shell is a user interface for the command line, called a command line interpreter.

It will interpret and execute commands on behalf of the user.

It also offers features such as a primitive programming language for scripting, wildcards, piping, shell variables (e.g. `PATH`), and more.

For example, we can redirect the output of one command as input to another command, such as the contents of the /etc/services file into the word count `wc` command and count the number of lines:

```
cat /etc/services | wc -l
```

Examples of shells on Unix-based operating systems include:

- `sh`
- `bash`
- `zsh`
- And so on.

On Windows, the shell is probably `cmd.exe`.

The shell is already running, it was probably used to start the Python program. We don't need to do anything special to get or have access to the shell.

Next, let's look at how we can run commands from asyncio as subprocesses.

How to Run a Command in a Subprocess

There are two ways to execute an external program as a subprocess in asyncio, they are:

- With `asyncio.create_subprocess_exec()`
- With `asyncio.create_subprocess_shell()`

Both functions return an `asyncio.subprocess.Process` object that represents the command running in a subprocess.

The `Process` object provides a handle on a subprocess in asyncio programs, allowing actions to be performed on it, such as waiting and terminating it.

Let's take a closer look at each of these functions in turn.

How to Run a Command Directly

The `asyncio.create_subprocess_exec()` function can be called to execute a command in a subprocess.

It returns a `Process` object as a handle on the subprocess.

The `create_subprocess_exec()` function is a coroutine and must be awaited. It will suspend the caller until the subprocess is started (not completed).

For example:

```
...
# run a command in a subprocess
process = await asyncio.create_subprocess_exec(
    'echo', 'Hello World')
```

We can configure the subprocess to receive input from the asyncio program or send output to the asyncio program by setting the `stdin`, `stdout`, and `stderr` arguments to the `asyncio.subprocess.PIPE` constant.

This will set the `stdin`, `stdout`, and `stderr` arguments on the `asyncio.subprocess.Process` to be a `StreamReader` or `StreamWriter` and allow coroutines to read or write from them via the `communicate()` method in the `Process` object, which we will explore further later.

For example:

```
...
# run a command in a subprocess
process = await asyncio.create_subprocess_exec(
```

```
'echo', 'Hello World',
stdout=asyncio.subprocess.PIPE)
```

We can explore how to get a `Process` instance by executing a command in a subprocess with the `create_subprocess_exec()` function.

The example below executes the `echo` command in a subprocess that prints out the provided string.

The subprocess is started, then the details of the subprocess are then reported.

The complete example is listed below.

```
# SuperFastPython.com
# example of running a command in a subprocess directly
import asyncio

# main coroutine
async def main():
    # run the command in a subprocess
    process = await asyncio.create_subprocess_exec(
        'echo', 'Hello World')
    # report the details of the subprocess
    print(f'subprocess: {process}')

# entry point
asyncio.run(main())
```

Running the example executes the echo command in a subprocess.

A `asyncio.subprocess.Process` instance is returned and the details are reported, showing the unique process id (PID).

The echo command then reports the provided string on `stdout`.

```
subprocess: <Process 50598>
Hello World
```

Next, let's look at an example of creating a subprocess via the shell.

How to Run a Command via the Shell

The `asyncio.create_subprocess_shell()` function can be called to execute a command in a subprocess.

The `create_subprocess_shell()` function will execute the provided command indirectly via the shell. This is the command line interpreter used to execute commands on the system, such as `bash` or `zsh` on Linux and macOS or `cmd.exe` on Windows.

Executing a command via the shell allows the capabilities of the shell to be used in addition to executing the command, such as wildcards and shell variables.

The function returns a `asyncio.subprocess.Process` as a handle on the subprocess.

The `create_subprocess_shell()` function is a coroutine and must be awaited. It will suspend the caller until the subprocess is started (not completed).

We can explore how to get a `Process` instance by executing a command in a subprocess with the `create_subprocess_shell()` function.

The example below executes the `echo` command in a subprocess that prints out the provided string. Unlike the `create_subprocess_exec()` function, the entire command with arguments is provided as a single string.

The subprocess is started, then the details of the subprocess are then reported.

The complete example is listed below.

```
# SuperFastPython.com
# example of running a cmd in a subprocess via the shell
import asyncio

# main coroutine
async def main():
    # run the command via shell in a subprocess
```

```
process = await asyncio.create_subprocess_shell(
    'echo Hello World')
# report the details of the subprocess
print(f'subprocess: {process}')

# entry point
asyncio.run(main())
```

Running the example executes the echo command in a subprocess.

A `asyncio.subprocess.Process` instance is returned and the details are reported, showing the unique process id (PID).

The echo command then reports the provided string on `stdout`.

```
subprocess: <Process 51822>
Hello World
```

Next, let's look at how we can wait for a subprocess to complete.

How to Wait for a Subprocess

We can wait for a subprocess to complete via the `wait()` method.

This is a coroutine that must be awaited.

The caller will be suspended until the subprocess is terminated, normally or otherwise.

If the subprocess is expecting input and is configured to receive input from our asyncio program via a pipe, then calling `wait()` can cause a deadlock as the caller cannot provide input to the subprocess if it is suspended.

For example:

```
...
# run a command in a subprocess
process = await asyncio.create_subprocess_shell(
    'sleep 3')
# wait for the subprocess to terminate
```

```
await process.wait()
```

Next, let's look at how we can read and write data from a subprocess.

How to Read and Write Data with a Subprocess

We can read data from a subprocess in asyncio via the communicate() method.

Reading data from the subprocess requires that the stdout or stderr arguments of the create_subprocess_shell() or create_subprocess_exec() functions was set to the PIPE constant.

No argument is provided and the method returns a tuple with input from stdout and stderr. Data is read until an end-of-file (EOF) character is received.

The communicate() method is a coroutine and must be awaited.

For example:

```
...
# run a command in a subprocess
process = await asyncio.create_subprocess_shell(
    'echo Hello World', stdout=asyncio.subprocess.PIPE)
# read data from the subprocess
data, _ = await process.communicate()
```

If no data can be read, the call will suspend until the subprocess has terminated.

We can write data to the subprocess from an asyncio coroutine also via the communicate() method. Data is provided via the input argument as bytes.

Writing data to the subprocess via the communicate() method requires that the stdin argument in the create_subprocess_shell() or create_subprocess_exec() functions were set to the PIPE constant.

For example:

```
...
# run a command in a subprocess
process = await asyncio.create_subprocess_exec(
    'cat', stdin=asyncio.subprocess.PIPE)
# write data to the subprocess
_ = await process.communicate(b'Hello World\n')
```

Next, let's look at how we can stop a command running in a subprocess.

How to Terminate and Kill a Subprocess

We can stop a subprocess via the `terminate()` method.

On most platforms, this sends a `SIGTERM` signal to the subprocess and terminates it immediately.

For example:

```
...
# terminate the subprocess
process.terminate()
```

We can also kill a subprocess via the `kill()` method.

On most platforms, this will send the `SIGKILL` signal to the subprocess in order to stop it immediately.

Unlike the `terminate()` method that sends the `SIGTERM` signal, the `SIGKILL` signal cannot be handled by the subprocess. This means it is assured to stop the subprocess.

For example:

```
...
# kill the subprocess
process.kill()
```

Next, let's move on from running commands from asyncio and explore how we can open and use non-blocking I/O streams.

How to Use Non-Blocking I/O Streams

Asyncio provides non-blocking I/O socket programming.

This is provided via streams.

Sockets can be opened that provide access to a stream writer and a stream reader.

Data can then be written and read from the stream using coroutines, suspending when appropriate.

Once finished, the socket can be closed.

The asyncio streams capability is low-level meaning that any protocols required must be implemented manually.

This can include common ASCII-based web protocols, such as:

- HTTP or HTTPS for interacting with web servers.
- SMTP for interacting with email servers.
- FTP for interacting with file servers.

The streams can also be used to create a server to handle requests using a standard protocol, or to develop our own application-specific protocol.

Now that we know what asyncio streams are, let's look at how to use them.

How to Open a Socket Connection

An asyncio TCP client socket connection can be opened using the `asyncio.open_connection()` function.

This is a coroutine that must be awaited and will return once the socket connection is open.

The function returns a `StreamReader` and `StreamWriter` object for interacting with the socket.

For example:

```
...
# open a connection
reader, writer = await asyncio.open_connection(...)
```

The `asyncio.open_connection()` function takes many arguments in order to configure the socket connection.

The two required arguments are the **host** and the **port**.

The **host** is a string that specifies the server to connect to, such as a domain name or an IP address.

The **port** is the socket port number, such as 80 for HTTP servers, 443 for HTTPS servers, 23 for SMTP and so on.

For example:

```
...
# open a connection to an http server
reader, writer = await asyncio.open_connection(
    'www.google.com', 80)
```

Encrypted socket connections are supported over the SSL protocol.

The most common example is HTTPS which is replacing HTTP.

This can be achieved by setting the **ssl** argument to **True**.

For example:

```
...
# open a connection to an https server
reader, writer = await asyncio.open_connection(
    'www.google.com', 443, ssl=True)
```

Next, let's look at how we can start a TCP server.

How to Start a TCP Server

An asyncio TCP server socket can be opened using the `asyncio.start_server()` function.

This is a coroutine that must be awaited.

The function returns an `asyncio.Server` object that represents the
running server.

For example:

```
...
# start a tcp server
server = await asyncio.start_server(...)
```

The three required arguments are the callback function, the host,
and the port.

The callback function is a custom function specified by name that
will be called each time a client connects to the server.

The host is the domain name or IP address that clients will specify
to connect. The port is the socket port number on which to receive
connections, such as 21 for FTP or 80 for HTTP.

For example:

```
# handle connections
async def handler(reader, writer):
    # ...

...
# start a server to receive http connections
server = await asyncio.start_server(
    handler, '127.0.0.1', 80)
```

Next, let's look at how we can write data to a stream.

How to Write Data with the `StreamWriter`

We can write data to the socket using an `asyncio.StreamWriter`.

Data is written as bytes.

Byte data can be written to the socket using the **write()** method.

For example:

```
...
# write byte data
writer.write(byte_data)
```

Alternatively, multiple *lines* of byte data organized into a list or iterable can be written using the `writelines()` method.

For example:

```
...
# write lines of byte data
writer.writelines(byte_lines)
```

Neither method for writing data suspends the calling coroutine.

After writing byte data it is a good idea to drain the socket via the `drain()` method.

This is a coroutine and will suspend the caller until the bytes have been transmitted and the socket is ready.

For example:

```
...
# write byte data
writer.write(byte_data)
# wait for data to be transmitted
await writer.drain()
```

String data can be converted into byte data for transmission by encoding it. This can be achieved using the `encode()` method on the string which will return byte data encoded with the default UTF8 encoding, ready for transmission.

For example:

```
...
# encode string data to byte data for transmission
byte_data = string_data.encode()
```

Next, let's look at how we can read data from a stream.

How to Read Data with the `StreamReader`

We can read data from the socket using an `asyncio.StreamReader`.

Data is read in byte format, therefore strings may need to be encoded before being used.

All read methods are coroutines that must be awaited.

An arbitrary number of bytes can be read via the `read()` method, which will read until the end of file (EOF).

```
...
# read byte data
byte_data = await reader.read()
```

Additionally, the number of bytes to read can be specified via the `n` argument.

This may be helpful if we know the number of bytes expected from the next response.

For example:

```
...
# read byte data
byte_data = await reader.read(n=100)
```

A single line of data can be read using the `readline()` method.

This will return bytes until a new line character `'\n'` is encountered, or EOF.

This is helpful when reading standard protocols that operate with lines of text.

```
...
# read a line data
byte_line = await reader.readline()
```

Additionally, there is a `readexactly()` method to read an exact number of bytes otherwise raise an exception, and a `readuntil()` that will read bytes until a specified character in byte form is read.

Data that is read from the stream can be decoded from bytes into string data using the `decode()` method and the default `UTF8` encoding.

For example:

```
...
# decode byte data into string data
string data = byte_data.decode()
```

Next, let's look at how we can close an open TCP socket connection.

How to Close the Socket Connection

The socket can be closed via the `asyncio.StreamWriter`.

The `close()` method can be called which will close the socket. This method does not suspend.

For example:

```
...
# close the socket
writer.close()
```

Although the `close()` method does not suspend, we can wait for the socket to close completely before continuing on.

This can be achieved via the `wait_closed()` method.

This is a coroutine that can be awaited.

For example:

```
...
# close the socket
writer.close()
# wait for the socket to close
await writer.wait_closed()
```

We can check if the socket has been closed or is in the process of being closed via the `is_closing()` method.

For example:

```
...
# check if the socket is closed or closing
if writer.is_closing():
    # ...
```

Now that we know how to open and use asyncio streams, let's look at a worked example of checking the status of webpages asynchronously.

Example of Checking Webpage Status

We can develop an example of checking the HTTP status of multiple webpages concurrently using non-blocking I/O.

This can be achieved by issuing an HTTP GET request to each webpage and reading the first line response which will contain the status of the webpage.

This requires first opening a socket connection to the HTTPS server on port 443 using SSL. We must then formulate the HTTP GET request that includes the URL we desire and the host name. The string request must then be encoded into byte data before being transmitted.

We can then read the first line of the response from the server, decode it and return it as the HTTP status of the server. The TCP socket can then be closed. This assumes the servers exist and that we can connect to it.

This process can be wrapped into a coroutine and executed concurrently for each website URL that we wish to query.

Tying this together, the complete example is listed below.

```
# SuperFastPython.com
# example of checking the status of multiple webpages
import asyncio
import urllib.parse

# get the http status of a webpage
async def get_status(url):
```

```python
    # split the url into components
    url_parsed = urllib.parse.urlsplit(url)
    # open the connection, assumes https
    reader, writer = await asyncio.open_connection(
        url_parsed.hostname, 443, ssl=True)
    # send GET request
    query = f'GET {url_parsed.path} HTTP/1.1\r\n' \
            f'Host: {url_parsed.hostname}\r\n\r\n'
    # write query to socket
    writer.write(query.encode())
    # wait for the bytes to be written to the socket
    await writer.drain()
    # read the single line response
    response = await reader.readline()
    # close the connection
    writer.close()
    # decode and strip white space
    status = response.decode().strip()
    # return the response
    return status

# main coroutine
async def main():
    # list of top 10 websites to check
    sites = ['https://www.google.com/',
             'https://www.youtube.com/',
             'https://www.facebook.com/',
             'https://twitter.com/',
             'https://www.instagram.com/',
             'https://www.baidu.com/',
             'https://www.wikipedia.org/',
             'https://yandex.ru/',
             'https://yahoo.com/',
             'https://www.whatsapp.com/']
    # create all coroutine requests
    coros = [get_status(url) for url in sites]
```

```
    # execute all coroutines and wait
    results = await asyncio.gather(*coros)
    # process all results
    for url, status in zip(sites, results):
        # report status
        print(f'{url:25}:\t{status}')

# run the asyncio program
asyncio.run(main())
```

Running the example first creates the `main()` coroutine and uses it as the entry point into the program.

The `main()` coroutine runs, defining a list of the top 10 websites to check.

A list of `get_status()` coroutines is created in a list comprehension, one coroutine per URL to check.

The `asyncio.gather()` function is then called, passing the coroutines and suspending the `main()` coroutine until they are all done.

The coroutines execute, querying each website concurrently and returning their status.

The `main()` coroutine resumes and receives an iterable of status values. This iterable along with the list of URLs is then traversed using the `zip()` built-in function and the statuses are reported.

This highlights how we can open, write to, and read from multiple TCP socket connections concurrently using non-blocking I/O.

```
https://www.google.com/    :  HTTP/1.1 200 OK
https://www.youtube.com/   :  HTTP/1.1 200 OK
https://www.facebook.com/:  HTTP/1.1 302 Found
https://twitter.com/       :  HTTP/1.1 200 OK
https://www.instagram.com/: HTTP/1.1 302 Found
https://www.baidu.com/     :  HTTP/1.1 200 OK
https://www.wikipedia.org/: HTTP/1.1 200 OK
https://yandex.ru/         :  HTTP/1.1 302 Moved ...
```

```
https://yahoo.com/         :  HTTP/1.1 301 Moved ...
https://www.whatsapp.com/:  HTTP/1.1 302 Found
```

Lesson Review

Takeaways

Well done, you made it to the end of the lesson.

- You now know how to run commands asynchronously as sub-processes directly from coroutines.
- You now know how to run commands asynchronously using the shell from coroutines.
- You now know how to open, read, and write from non-blocking TCP socket connections.
- You now know how to check the status of webpages asynchronously using streams.

Exercise

Your task for this lesson is to expand upon the example that checks website status.

Update the example to check the status of specific webpages you read often.

Further update the example to read the entire HTTP header for each URL and report details from the header, at least the number of characters. This can be achieved by reading lines until the first double new line is encountered.

Further update the example to read the HTTP body of the response and report interesting details, such as the number of characters. The body begins right after the header finishes with a double new line.

The structure of HTTP response messages is very simple. The Wikipedia page for HTTP contains examples of request and response messages if you are stuck.

This is an important exercise as it will force you to get comfortable reading data from socket connections and interpreting the messages in the context of an application domain.

Share your results online on Twitter, LinkedIn, GitHub, or similar.

Send me the link to your results, I'd love to see what you come up with.

You can send me a message directly via:

- Super Fast Python - Contact Page
  https://SuperFastPython.com/contact/

Or share it with me on Twitter via @SuperFastPython.

Further Reading

This section provides resources for you to learn more about the topics covered in this lesson.

- `asyncio` - Asynchronous I/O.
  https://docs.python.org/3/library/asyncio.html
- Asyncio Subprocesses.
  https://docs.python.org/3/library/asyncio-subprocess.html
- Asyncio Streams.
  https://docs.python.org/3/library/asyncio-stream.html
- Hypertext Transfer Protocol, Wikipedia.
  https://en.wikipedia.org/wiki/Hypertext_Transfer_Protocol

Next

In the next lesson, we will explore how to draw upon everything we have learned and develop an asynchronous and concurrent port scanning program using asyncio.

Lesson 07: Port Scanner Case Study

Asyncio coroutines can be used to scan multiple ports on a server concurrently. This can dramatically speed up the process compared to attempting to connect to each port, one by one. In this lesson, we will explore how to develop a concurrent port scanner with asyncio.

After completing this tutorial, you will know:

- How to open a socket connection to each port sequentially and how slow it can be.
- How to execute coroutines concurrently to scan ports and wait for them to complete.
- How to scan port numbers concurrently and report results dynamically as soon as they are available.

Let's get started.

Develop an Asyncio Port Scanner

We can connect to other computers by opening a socket, called socket programming.

Opening a socket requires both the name or IP address of the server and a port number on which to connect.

For example, when our web browser opens a web page on python.org, it is opening a socket connection to that server on port 80 or 443, then uses the HTTP protocol to request and download (GET) an HTML file.

Socket programming or network programming is a lot of fun.

A good first socket programming project is to develop a port scanner. This is a program that reports all of the open sockets on a given server.

A simple way to implement a port scanner is to loop over all the ports we want to test and attempt to make a socket connection on each. If a connection can be made, we disconnect immediately and report that the port on the server is open.

Historically, having many open ports on a server was a security risk, so it is common to lock down a public-facing server and close all non-essential ports to external traffic. This means scanning public servers will likely yield few open ports in the best case or will deny future access in the worst case if the server thinks we're trying to break in.

As such, although developing a port scanner is a fun socket programming exercise, we must be careful in how we use it and what servers we scan.

Next, let's look at how we can open a socket connection on a single port.

How to Open a Socket Connection on a Port

We can open a socket connection in asyncio using the `asyncio.open_connection()` function.

This takes the host and port number and returns a **StreamReader** and **StreamWriter** for interacting with the server via the socket.

The `asyncio.open_connection()` function is a coroutine and must be awaited. It will return once the connection is open.

For example:

```
...
# open a socket connection
reader, writer = asyncio.open_connection(
    'python.org', 80)
```

If a connection can be made, the port is open. Otherwise, if the connection cannot be made, the port is not open.

The problem is, how do we know a connection cannot be made?

If a port is not open, the call may wait for a long time before giving up. We need a way to give up after a time limit.

This can be achieved using the `asyncio.wait_for()` function.

This is a coroutine that will execute an awaitable and wait a fixed interval in seconds before giving up and raising an `asyncio.TimeoutError` exception.

We can create the coroutine for the `asyncio.open_connection()` function and pass it to the `wait_for()` coroutine.

This will allow us to attempt to make a socket connection on a given port for a fixed interval, such as one or three seconds.

For example:

```
...
# create coroutine for opening a connection
coro = asyncio.open_connection('python.org', 80)
# execute the coroutine with a timeout
try:
    # open the connection and wait for a moment
    _ = await asyncio.wait_for(coro, 1.0)
    # ...
except asyncio.TimeoutError:
    # ...
```

If the connection can be made within the time limit we can then close the connection.

This can be achieved by calling the close() method on the StreamWriter object returned from asyncio.open_connection().

For example:

```
...
# close connection once opened
writer.close()
```

Otherwise, if the asyncio.TimeoutError exception is raised, we can assume that the port is probably not open.

We can tie all of this together into a coroutine function that tests one port on one host and returns True if the port is open or False otherwise.

The test_port_number() coroutine function below implements this.

```
# returns True if a connection can be made
async def test_port_number(host, port, timeout=3):
    # create coroutine for opening a connection
    coro = asyncio.open_connection(host, port)
    # execute the coroutine with a timeout
    try:
        # open the connection and wait for a moment
        _,writer = await asyncio.wait_for(coro, timeout)
        # close connection once opened
        writer.close()
        # indicate the connection can be opened
        return True
    except asyncio.TimeoutError:
        # indicate the connection cannot be opened
        return False
```

Next, let's look at how we can scan a large number of ports, one by one.

How to Scan a Range of Ports on a Server (*slow*)

We can scan a range of ports on a given host.

Many common internet services are provided on ports between 0 and 1,024.

The viable range of ports is 0 to 65,535, and we can see a list of the most common port numbers and the services that use them in the file `/etc/services` on POSIX systems.

We can scan a range of ports by repeatedly calling our coroutine developed in the previous section, and report any ports that permit a connection as *open*.

The `main()` coroutine function below implements this reporting any open ports that are discovered.

```python
# main coroutine
async def main(host, ports):
    # report a status message
    print(f'Scanning {host}...')
    # scan ports sequentially
    for port in ports:
        if await test_port_number(host, port):
            print(f'> {host}:{port} [OPEN]')
```

Finally, we can call this function and specify the host and range of ports.

In this case, we will port scan `python.org` (out of love for Python, not malicious intent).

```python
...
# define a host and ports to scan
host = 'python.org'
ports = range(1, 1024)
# start the asyncio program
asyncio.run(main(host, ports))
```

We would expect that at least port 80 would be open for HTTP connections.

Tying this together, the complete example of port scanning a host with asyncio is listed below.

```
# SuperFastPython.com
# example of an asyncio sequential port scanner
import asyncio

# returns True if a connection can be made
async def test_port_number(host, port, timeout=3):
    # create coroutine for opening a connection
    coro = asyncio.open_connection(host, port)
    # execute the coroutine with a timeout
    try:
        # open the connection and wait for a moment
        _,writer = await asyncio.wait_for(coro, timeout)
        # close connection once opened
        writer.close()
        # indicate the connection can be opened
        return True
    except asyncio.TimeoutError:
        # indicate the connection cannot be opened
        return False

# main coroutine
async def main(host, ports):
    # report a status message
    print(f'Scanning {host}...')
    # scan ports sequentially
    for port in ports:
        if await test_port_number(host, port):
            print(f'> {host}:{port} [OPEN]')

# define a host and ports to scan
host = 'python.org'
ports = range(1, 1024)
```

```
# start the asyncio program
asyncio.run(main(host, ports))
```

Running the example attempts to make a connection for each port number between 1 and 1,023 (one minus 1,024) and reports all open ports.

In this case, we can see that port 80 for HTTP is open as expected, and port 443 is also open for HTTPS.

The program works fine, but it is painfully slow.

On my system, it took about 51 minutes. This makes sense. If we test 1,023 ports and most ports are closed then we expect to wait 3 seconds on each attempt or $1,023 \times 3$ which equals 3,069 seconds. Converting this to minutes $\frac{3069}{60}$ equals about 51.15 minutes.

```
> python.org:80 [OPEN]
> python.org:443 [OPEN]
```

The benefit of asyncio is that it can execute coroutines concurrently, specifically coroutines that perform non-blocking I/O.

Next, we will look at how to run coroutines concurrently to speed up this port scanning process.

How to Scan Ports Concurrently (*fast*)

We can scan ports concurrently using asyncio.

Each port can be tested concurrently in a separate coroutine.

Opening a connection will suspend the caller, allowing other coroutines to run. Those coroutines attempting to connect to a port that is not open will remain suspended until the time out elapses, allowing other coroutines to run.

This can be implemented by creating one coroutine for each port to scan, then execute all coroutines concurrently and wait for them to complete. This can be achieved using the `asyncio.gather()` function.

It requires first creating the coroutines. With one coroutine per port, this would be a collection of more than 1,000 coroutines. We can achieve this using a list comprehension.

For example:

```
...
# create all coroutines
coros = [test_port_number(host, port) for port in ports]
```

Next, we can execute all of these coroutines concurrently using the `asyncio.gather()` function.

This function takes awaitables as arguments and will not return until the awaitables are complete. It does not take a list of awaitables, therefore we must expand our list into separate expressions using the star (*) operator.

For example:

```
...
# execute all coroutines concurrently
results = await asyncio.gather(*coros)
```

This will execute all coroutines concurrently and will return an iterable of return values from each coroutine in the order provided.

We can then traverse the list of return values along with the list of ports and report the results.

Recall that we can traverse two or more iterables together using the built-in `zip()` function.

For example:

```
...
# report results
for port,result in zip(ports, results):
    if result :
        print(f'> {host}:{port} [OPEN]')
```

Tying this together, the complete example is listed below.

```python
# SuperFastPython.com
# example of a concurrent port scanner using gather
import asyncio

# returns True if a connection can be made
async def test_port_number(host, port, timeout=3):
    # create coroutine for opening a connection
    coro = asyncio.open_connection(host, port)
    # execute the coroutine with a timeout
    try:
        # open the connection and wait for a moment
        _,writer = await asyncio.wait_for(coro, timeout)
        # close connection once opened
        writer.close()
        # indicate the connection can be opened
        return True
    except asyncio.TimeoutError:
        # indicate the connection cannot be opened
        return False

# main coroutine
async def main(host, ports):
    # report a status message
    print(f'Scanning {host}...')
    # create all coroutines
    coros = [test_port_number(host, port)
        for port in ports]
    # execute all coroutines concurrently
    results = await asyncio.gather(*coros)
    # report results
    for port,result in zip(ports, results):
        if result :
            print(f'> {host}:{port} [OPEN]')

# define a host and ports to scan
```

```
host = 'python.org'
ports = range(1, 1024)
# start the asyncio program
asyncio.run(main(host, ports))
```

Running the example executes the `main()` coroutine as the entry point into our asyncio program.

A list of coroutines is first created.

The coroutines are then all executed concurrently using `asyncio.gather()`.

This suspends the `main()` coroutine until all coroutines are completed. Each coroutine tests one port, attempting to open a connection and suspending it until either the connection is open or the timeout is elapsed.

Once all tasks are completed the `main()` coroutine resumes and all results are reported.

Two open ports are reported the same as before.

The big difference is the speed of execution. In this case, it takes about 3.1 seconds, compared to more than 50 minutes in the previous example.

That is about 3,063 seconds faster or a 989x speed-up, i.e. nearly 1000-times faster.

```
Scanning python.org...
> python.org:80 [OPEN]
> python.org:443 [OPEN]
```

Next, let's look at how we can report results as soon as they are available, rather than after all coroutines complete.

How to Report Scan Results Dynamically

In the previous example, we executed the coroutines concurrently and reported the results after all tasks had been completed.

An alternative approach would be to report results as the tasks are completed.

This would allow the program to be more responsive and show results to the user as they are available.

We could achieve this by having the `test_port_number()` coroutine report its result directly.

Another approach is to traverse coroutines in the order they are completed, as they complete.

This can be achieved using the `asyncio.as_completed()` function.

This function takes a collection of awaitables. If they are coroutines, they are issued as tasks.

The function then returns an iterable of the coroutines that are yielded in the order that they are completed.

We can traverse this iterable directly, we do not need to use the `async for` expression reserved for asynchronous iterables.

For example:

```
...
# execute coroutines and handle results as they complete
for coro in asyncio.as_completed(coros):
    # check the return value from the coroutine
        # ...
```

The downside is that we don't have an easy way to relate the coroutine to the port that was tested. Therefore, we can update our `test_port_number()` coroutine to return whether the port is open and the port number that was tested.

For example:

```
# returns True if a connection can be made
async def test_port_number(host, port, timeout=3):
    # create coroutine for opening a connection
    coro = asyncio.open_connection(host, port)
    # execute the coroutine with a timeout
    try:
        # open the connection and wait for a moment
        _,writer = await asyncio.wait_for(coro, timeout)
        # close connection once opened
        writer.close()
        # indicate the connection can be opened
        return True,port
    except asyncio.TimeoutError:
        # indicate the connection cannot be opened
        return False,port
```

We can then traverse the coroutines in the order they are completed and get the details of the port and whether it is open from each and report it.

For example:

```
...
# execute coroutines and handle results as they complete
for coro in asyncio.as_completed(coros):
    # check the return value from the coroutine
    result, port = await coro
    if result:
        print(f'> {host}:{port} [OPEN]')
```

This will execute all coroutines concurrently and will report open ports as they are discovered, rather than all at the end.

Tying this together, the complete example is listed below.

```
# SuperFastPython.com
# example concurrent port scanner using as_completed
import asyncio
```

```python
# returns True if a connection can be made
async def test_port_number(host, port, timeout=3):
    # create coroutine for opening a connection
    coro = asyncio.open_connection(host, port)
    # execute the coroutine with a timeout
    try:
        # open the connection and wait for a moment
        _,writer = await asyncio.wait_for(coro, timeout)
        # close connection once opened
        writer.close()
        # indicate the connection can be opened
        return True,port
    except asyncio.TimeoutError:
        # indicate the connection cannot be opened
        return False,port

# main coroutine
async def main(host, ports):
    # report a status message
    print(f'Scanning {host}...')
    # create all coroutines
    coros = [test_port_number(host, port)
        for port in ports]
    # execute coroutines and handle results dynamically
    for coro in asyncio.as_completed(coros):
        # check the return value from the coroutine
        result, port = await coro
        if result:
            print(f'> {host}:{port} [OPEN]')

# define a host and ports to scan
host = 'python.org'
ports = range(1, 1024)
# start the asyncio program
asyncio.run(main(host, ports))
```

Running the example executes the **main()** coroutine as the entry point into the asyncio program.

A list of coroutines is first created.

The coroutines are then passed to the `asyncio.as_completed()` function.

This wraps each in another coroutine and executes them all concurrently and independently.

It returns immediately with an iterable of coroutines.

Internally, it awaits and yields coroutines as they are completed.

The return value from each coroutine is retrieved and results are reported as they are made available.

The example shows the same ports and executes in about the same time as the previous concurrent examples, except the program is more responsive.

Ports are shown as open almost immediately, as opposed to after all ports in the range have been checked and timed out.

```
Scanning python.org...
> python.org:80 [OPEN]
> python.org:443 [OPEN]
```

Lesson Review

Takeaways

Well done, you made it to the end of the lesson.

- You now know how to open a socket connection to each port sequentially and how slow it can be.
- You now know how to execute coroutines concurrently to scan ports and wait for them to complete.
- You now know how to scan port numbers concurrently and report results dynamically as soon as they are available.

Exercise

Your task for this lesson is to extend the above example for port scanning.

1. Update the example to test a different range of port numbers.
2. Update the example to test the program on a different host that has more than two ports open.
3. Update the concurrent example to use `asyncio.wait()` instead of `asyncio.gather()`.
4. Update the example to limit the number of concurrent tasks using a fixed sized queue or a semaphore.
5. Update the example so that if an HTTP or HTTPS port is open that it reports the HTTP status for the port.

It is important that you know how to use the non-blocking I/O aspect of asyncio in conjunction with the tools provided in the `asyncio` module. The above example and these extensions will help you get comfortable with these tools in this specific use case.

Share your results online on Twitter, LinkedIn, GitHub, or similar.

Send me the link to your results, I'd love to see what you come up with.

You can send me a message directly via:

- Super Fast Python - Contact Page
  https://SuperFastPython.com/contact/

Or share it with me on Twitter via @SuperFastPython.

Further Reading

This section provides resources for you to learn more about the topics covered in this lesson.

- `asyncio` - Asynchronous I/O.
  https://docs.python.org/3/library/asyncio.html
- Asyncio Streams.
  https://docs.python.org/3/library/asyncio-stream.html

- Network socket, Wikipedia.
  https://en.wikipedia.org/wiki/Network_socket
- Computer network programming, Wikipedia.
  https://en.wikipedia.org/wiki/Computer_network_programming
- Port scanner, Wikipedia.
  https://en.wikipedia.org/wiki/Port_scanner

Next

This was the last lesson, next we will take a look back at how far we have come.

Conclusions

Look Back At How Far You've Come

Congratulations, you made it to the end of this 7-day course.

Let's take a look back and review what you now know.

- You discovered how to define, create, and run coroutines and how to use the `async`/`await` expressions.
- You discovered how to create asynchronous tasks, query their status, cancel them and add callback functions.
- You discovered how to run many coroutines concurrently in a group and handle their results.
- You discovered how to wait for many coroutines to complete, meet a condition, or timeout.
- You discovered how to define, create and use asynchronous iterators, generators, and context managers.
- You discovered how to use the `async for` and `async with` expressions in asyncio programs.
- You discovered how to synchronize and coordinate coroutines with locks, semaphores, events and condition variables.
- You discovered how to share data between coroutines using coroutine-safe queues.
- You discovered how to run, read, and write from subprocesses and streams with coroutines.
- You discovered how to develop a concurrent and dynamically updating port scanner using non-blocking I/O.

You now know how to use the `asyncio` module and bring coroutine-based concurrency to your project.

Thank you for letting me help you on your journey into Python concurrency.

Jason Brownlee, Ph.D.
SuperFastPython.com
2022.

Resources For Diving Deeper

This section lists some useful additional resources for further reading.

APIs

- Concurrent Execution API - Python Standard Library.
  https://docs.python.org/3/library/concurrency.html
- `multiprocessing` API - Process-based parallelism.
  https://docs.python.org/3/library/multiprocessing.html
- `threading` API - Thread-based parallelism.
  https://docs.python.org/3/library/threading.html
- `concurrent.futures` API - Launching parallel tasks.
  https://docs.python.org/3/library/concurrent.futures.html
- `asyncio` API - Asynchronous I/O.
  https://docs.python.org/3/library/asyncio.html

Books

- High Performance Python, Ian Ozsvald, et al., 2020.
  https://amzn.to/3wRD5MX
- Using AsyncIO in Python, Caleb Hattingh, 2020.
  https://amzn.to/3lNp2ml
- Python Concurrency with asyncio, Matt Fowler, 2022.
  https://amzn.to/3LZvxNn
- Effective Python, Brett Slatkin, 2019.
  https://amzn.to/3GpopJ1

- Python Cookbook, David Beazley, et al., 2013.
  https://amzn.to/3MSFzBv
- Python in a Nutshell, Alex Martelli, et al., 2017.
  https://amzn.to/3m7SLGD

Getting More Help

Do you have any questions?

Below provides some great places online where you can ask questions about Python programming and Python concurrency:

- Stack Overview.
  https://stackoverflow.com/
- Python Subreddit.
  https://www.reddit.com/r/python
- LinkedIn Python Developers Community.
  https://www.linkedin.com/groups/25827
- Quora Python (programming language).
  https://www.quora.com/topic/Python-programming-language-1

Contact the Author

You are not alone.

If you ever have any questions about the lessons in this book, please contact me directly:

- Super Fast Python - Contact Page
  https://SuperFastPython.com/contact/

I will do my best to help.

About the Author

Jason Brownlee, Ph.D. helps Python developers bring modern concurrency methods to their projects with hands-on tutorials. Learn more at SuperFastPython.com.

Jason is a software engineer and research scientist with a background in artificial intelligence and high-performance computing. He has authored more than 20 technical books on machine learning and has built, operated, and exited online businesses.

Figure 1: Photo of Jason Brownlee

Python Concurrency Jump-Start Series

Save days of debugging with step-by-step jump-start guides.

Python Threading Jump-Start.
https://SuperFastPython.com/ptj

Python ThreadPool Jump-Start.
https://SuperFastPython.com/ptpj

Python ThreadPoolExecutor Jump-Start.
https://SuperFastPython.com/ptpej

Python Multiprocessing Jump-Start.
https://SuperFastPython.com/pmj

Python Multiprocessing Pool Jump-Start.
https://SuperFastPython.com/pmpj

Python ProcessPoolExecutor Jump-Start.
https://SuperFastPython.com/pppej

Python Asyncio Jump-Start.
https://SuperFastPython.com/paj

Made in the USA
Middletown, DE
08 July 2025

10283742R00106